THE HISTORY OF MORDEN COLLEGE

Patronage and Poverty in
Merchant Society

THE HISTORY

OF

MORDEN COLLEGE

BLACKHEATH

1695 to the Present

PATRICK JOYCE

Published by

GRESHAM BOOKS

in association with

THE TRUSTEES OF MORDEN COLLEGE

FIRST PUBLISHED 1982

© TRUSTEES OF MORDEN COLLEGE 1982
BLACKHEATH, LONDON SE3

ISBN 0905418 913

GRESHAM BOOKS

The Gresham Press, P.O. Box 61
Henley-on-Thames, Oxfordshire RG9 3LQ

Designed, Printed and Bound by
STAPLES PRINTERS ST ALBANS LIMITED
at The Priory Press, Hertfordshire

to the members of Morden College
past and present

Author's Introduction and Acknowledgements

This book was designed to be read by historians and other scholars, by those involved in the College and interested in its history, and by readers with a less specialised and direct interest in the topics taken up for discussion. Most of the argument and debate that will concern those in the field of historical enquiry will be found in one chapter, chapter two. Thus, though this chapter informs the direction and content of the rest of the book, those whose primary concern is with the history of Morden College, or with the history of similar institutions, will probably find that the complete narrative history in the remaining chapters corresponds most closely to their interests. Those, 'specialists' or otherwise, who are interested in the history of charity, the nature of London mercantile society, the social role of patronage, and in the poverty of the 'gentle' poor, may find chapter two the best introduction to the work as a whole. The themes developed here are interwoven with the narrative, and subjected to examination in the light of the detailed reconstruction of this single institution's history. If there are disadvantages in looking at a single, unique institution then there are also advantages: the concrete detail revealed in the College's unusually extensive archives enables matters hitherto neglected to be at least opened for further consideration.

All institutions – the Crown, Parliament, the City – have changed greatly over the centuries, and Morden College is no exception to this rule. The even tenor of College life in the present, comfortable and well-liked by the College members, contrasts with the years before the turn of the present century. This change receives detailed consideration in chapters five and six. Thus the distinction between past and present is amply evidenced in the history that follows; though, by definition in a work of scholarly history on a seventeenth-century institution, it is the long period of the old order in College life that absorbs most attention.

It was in these years that the terms of our title were most appropriate, and again the contrast between past and present is apparent: until the twentieth century the links between social authority, patronage and charity in merchant society were close. Nonetheless, the emphasis placed upon power and influence in the dispensation of charity does not exhaust the meaning of the social work-ings of charity nor fully account for the diversity of motive in the charitable patron. This point is made in the course of chapter two, where it is seen that patrons gave from a variety of motives, many of them noble and generous. Yet the motives for giving, the conditions attaching to charitable acts, and the conse-quences of these acts, all have to be understood in their historical context and not solely in terms of the charitable patrons' own ideas of their acts and the consequences of these acts. It is this that chapter two attempts. Past charity is historically understandable only when it is interpreted in terms of contemporary social structure, and ideas about the social and religious order, ideas that are never the same as our own. When charity is viewed in terms of what merchants felt about themselves and the society around them, and especially what they felt about wealth and poverty, then the full force of influence and patronage in merchant charitable provision and merchant life becomes apparent. Only when it is apparent – and this book is as much, and more, about the recipients as the donors of charity – can we go on to explore the experience of poverty, and know what Morden College was in the past, how it came to be founded and why it was run in the way it was. No single historical account can claim a monopoly of the truth. All that may be hoped is that the historian's chosen viewpoint does a little more justice to the past than had been done before.

This work was commissioned by the trustees of Morden College, acting in conjunction with the Institute of Historical Research, University of London. I should like to thank Sir Ralph Perring, currently chairman of the College trustees, for his unfailing courtesy and enthusiasm. I should also like to thank the College Archivist, Miss I. Dyer, for her invaluable assistance. The staff and members of Morden College were invariably helpful, friendly and interested, and I take this opportunity of thanking them for making my time at the College so pleasant. Professor F. M. L. Thompson and Mr. William Kellaway, respectively Director and Librarian of the Institute of Historical Research, were liberal with their advice and support. My gratitude too to Miss Christina Gray and Miss Angela White for their pains in the typing of the manuscript.

Manchester 1982.

Foreword

The Trustees of Morden College were left a sum of money by Dr Hazel Mews on condition that they published in consultation with the Institute of Historical Research a scholarly history of the College. Dr Mews, who was a resident in the College, had intended to write the history herself, but unfortunately died before she could attempt the task. After discussion, Dr Patrick Joyce was nominated to be the author and spent a full year on research in the College Archives. For the first time there are published the names of all the Trustees, the Chaplains, the Treasurers and Clerks to the Trustees who have formed the administration over the years. These cover the period of original trusteeship, the Turkey Company, the East India Company and for the past 98 years the Court of Aldermen of The City of London, and the Trustees thank Dr Joyce for putting on record an interesting account of the personalities who have been involved.

In a work of this nature dealing with the subject of charity there is necessarily scope for differences in both interpretation of events and viewpoint. While the Trustees do not fully agree with every one of the author's comments and opinions, they feel it is important the history should be published as provided for in Dr Mew's bequest.

The residents, the pensioners, the Trustees and the staff of the College are intensely proud of the heritage that has been passed down to them from Sir John and Lady Morden; it is rewarding to read of the events that have formed its history through nearly three hundred years.

Ralph Perring.

Chairman and Honorary Treasurer

Trustees of Morden College

x

Contents

AUTHOR'S INTRODUCTION AND ACKNOWLEDGEMENTS

FOREWORD BY THE CHAIRMAN AND HONORARY TREASURER

LIST OF PRESENT TRUSTEES

Chapter One – page 1
SIR JOHN MORDEN AND THE FOUNDATION OF MORDEN COLLEGE

Chapter Two – page 11
MERCHANTS PROSPEROUS AND MERCHANTS DECAYED:
CHARITY AND GENTEEL POVERTY IN LONDON

Chapter Three – page 31
ESTATE AND COLLEGE FINANCE AND MANAGEMENT

Chapter Four – page 43
THE WORLD OF MORDEN COLLEGE I:
THE TURKEY COMPANY PERIOD 1708–1826

Chapter Five – page 61
THE WORLD OF MORDEN COLLEGE II:
THE EAST INDIA COMPANY PERIOD 1827–1884

Chapter Six – page 81
THE WORLD OF MORDEN COLLEGE III:
THE CITY ALDERMEN PERIOD 1884 TO THE PRESENT

Appendices – pages 97 to 106
A NOTE ON THE ARCHITECTURE OF MORDEN COLLEGE

A NOTE ON SOURCES

LIST OF TRUSTEES AND OFFICERS OF MORDEN COLLEGE

Sir John Morden, Baronet
1623–1708
Founder of Morden College

From an original painting by Sir Peter Lely at the College

Lady Susan Morden
1638–1721
Wife of Sir John Morden

From an original painting by Sir Peter Lely at the College

An Anagram & Acrostick in Memory of the Hono:ble
Sr. IOHN MORDEN, of WRICKLEMARCH in ye County
of KENT Baronet, The Founder of this Blessed Worke
of Charity for Decayed Merchants An° Domi 1695.
The Anagram is I HONOR MEND

I ICANNOT GIVE A FAIRER CHARACTER
O OF HIM THEN WHAT HIS ACTIONS DO INFER
H HOW BRIGHT AN ASPECT HATH THIS CHARITY
N NOTHING CAN SHINE WITH GREATER ORIENCY.
M MOST STRIVE TO RIVAL HEAV'N IN Power & BE
O ON TERMS OF Grandeur LIKE THE DEITIE
R REGARDLES OF THOSE BEAMES OF MAJESTIE,
D DO FROM TRUE GOODNES SPRING To Glory tend,
E Exceeding Alms WIL FORTH ITS ODOURS SEND
N NONE BUT THE GOOD CAN SAY I Honor mend.

Anagram and acrostic engraved on stone in praise of
Sir John Morden. This plaque is situated in the
Quadrangle of the College

CHAPTER ONE

Sir John Morden and the Foundation of Morden College

Morden College, sited at the south-eastern edge of London's Blackheath, was founded by the Levant Company and East India Company merchant Sir John Morden in 1695, and built between 1695 and 1700 to a design attributed to Sir Christopher Wren. Administered by the founder until his death in 1708, by the terms of his will administrative responsibility thereafter devolved upon trustees chosen from the Levant (or Turkey) Company (1708–1826), the East India Company (1827–84), and from 1884 to the present the Court of Aldermen of the City of London.[1] The College was founded as a home for elderly and 'decayed' merchants and long retained its mercantile character. As the only institution of its sort in the country its history is of considerable importance in interpreting the nature of eighteenth- and nineteenth-century London mercantile society. The donation and receipt of charity among this section of the community also throws light upon the changing complexion of the City over the centuries. Above all, perhaps, it leads us into a significant area of enquiry, largely unregarded by historians, that of respectable or genteel poverty.

Sir John Morden himself was born in London in 1623, the baptism being registered at St Bride's Church, Fleet Street, in that year. In the following year his father, George Morden, was buried in St Bride's Churchyard, the register describing him as a 'housekeeper and working fellow, and free'.[2] As a goldsmith and City freeman George Morden was clearly a man of some substance: he left legacies of £450 to both his son and daughter. Of John Morden's early career little is known until his return from the East around 1660 with a 'fair estate' amassed by trading as a Turkey merchant.[3] Though born into the *milieu* of City commercial life – there was a close connection between banking and the goldsmith's craft at the time – Morden had clearly transcended his relatively humble origins by the time of his return to England. His standing then was both reflected and increased by his marriage in 1662 to Susan Brand, the daughter of a well-to-do Suffolk family long ensconced in their country seat at Edwardstone, and carrying on a prosperous business as wool merchants and clothiers in London and Suffolk as well. By Susan Morden's time (1638–1721) members of the family lived in great comfort in the City, near to the markets and the river.[4]

The marriage brought John Morden into the social and political world of the

1

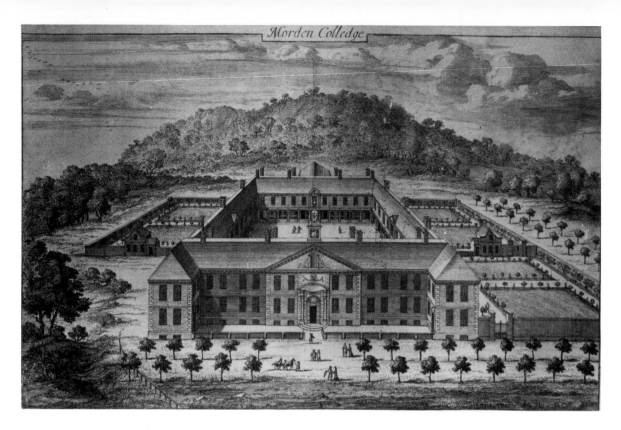

Morden Colledge

Morden College, Blackheath

**Published according to Act of Parliament, 1755
for John Stow's *Survey of London***

Sir Christopher Wren, 1632–1723,

Whose association with John Morden certainly dated before 1691 through the East India Company. (See first edition of *Ceylon* by Robert Knox, published 1691).

The College was built to a design attributed to Wren

great London merchants. The ramifications of the Brand pedigree indicate the central importance of marriage as a means of economic organisation and social coherence in mercantile society. Susan Morden's father, Joseph Brand, had married Thomasin, daughter of the London merchant Thomas Trotter, and from this union marriage alliances in the next generation were forged between one of the Brand sisters and Sir Samuel Barnardiston, Baronet, of Brightwell Hall in Suffolk; between another sister and Sir John Bennett, Sargeant-at-law and Judge of the Marshalsea Court; and between one of the Brand brothers and a daughter of Sir Thomas Barnardiston. Sir Samuel and Sir Thomas Barnardiston were foremost among the Puritan merchants and Whig parliamentarians of the seventeenth century. The family traded as Turkey merchants in Aleppo and Smyrna. Sir Samuel became Deputy Governor of the East India Company in 1668, one means among many by which he amassed a considerable fortune. Both brothers, like their father, were active Cromwellians, Sir Thomas assisting Cromwell's forces with a regiment of foot in 1648 and sitting as Cromwellian M.P. for Suffolk.[5]

To what extent the foundations of the Morden marriage as well as the Morden fortune were laid in the East is unclear: the Barnardistons traded in the Levant at the same time as Sir John Morden, and quite likely helped him to connection as well as wealth in those years. The county connection probably mattered too: Morden's grandfather was a Suffolk man, though of humbler station than the squirearchical Barnardistons and Brands. Morden's progress after the marriage was considerable enough to surround his name with legend, an accretion that time has done little to dispel. The story of his lost ships, his reduction to a butcher's boy in the interim, his vow to build Morden College if his ships were returned to him, and the miraculous return of the vessels after ten years is a reflection rather of the City's own mythology of success and providential inspiration than of the truth, though none the less interesting for that.[6] The Barnardiston connection was of somewhat more substance: after his return to London Morden carried on business in Bishopsgate, as did the Barnardistons. W. K. Jordan has shown how around this time the society of the great London merchants was unified not only by marriage but by the common experience of apprenticeship, especially in the great chartered companies like the Turkey Company, and by a common business and residential situation in the City.[7]

By the early part of the eighteenth century the big merchants were increasingly making use of the country house as a place of retreat, and, after the improvements in the conditions of the road system after mid-century, as a daily rather than a weekend haven.[8] The Greenwich and Blackheath area, with fairly easy access to the City, seems to have been in the van of this change: in the 1720s Daniel Defoe described Greenwich as a place of genteel retirement, the town bursting its bounds as the landed and military classes, as well as businessmen involved in the local naval yards and ordnance, chose it as the site of residence or retirement.[9] In this process of colonisation John Morden was among the first to see the advantages of the area. In 1669 he purchased the Wricklemarsh estate in the parish of Charlton for £4,200, an old gentry seat with a two-hundred-acre park and a mansion. Morden did not, however, settle at Wricklemarsh to retire, for he carried on business in the City for over three decades after moving there. As Defoe put it, 'the beauty of Greenwich is owing to the lustre of its inhabitants, where there is a kind of collection of gentlemen, rather than citizens . . .', and (to the son of a 'citizen') not the least of the advantages of local residence in earlier years was the Court Charles II held at the Queen's House, Greenwich, towards the end of his reign. Though there is no record of the Mordens attending Court, under William and Mary they would certainly have mixed with the local gentry and Court elements by virtue of Sir John Morden's appointment as one of a commission of Survey of His Majesty's Lordship of the Manor of Greenwich. In 1698 he further increased his stature as a landed gentleman by purchasing the Manor of Old Court for £9,000. It is not without significance that one John Thompson, 'Yeoman of the mouth', or royal cook and taster to four English sovereigns, ended his days in the household of this paragon of commercial virtue and success.

The London mercantile oligarchy of the late seventeenth century was both receptive to authoritative and patriarchal concepts of society, and sympathetic to a monarchy upon which it depended for its company charters. In the Civil War itself the greater merchants either sided with the King or were neutral, religious conviction (and remembered grievance) providing a limited number of exceptions to the rule.[10] Among the latter were to be numbered the Barnardistons, and they were in due time to welcome the Restoration, a welcome for which they were to be speedily rewarded by royal favour (Thomas Barnardiston was given his baronetcy in 1663). In running with the hare and hunting with the hounds John Morden was no less adept than most of his class: he was made a baronet by James II three months before the King's impecunious flight in 1688, and in 1691 appointed a Commissioner of Excise under William III. After the Glorious Revolution, and the financial 'revolution' that accompanied it and consolidated the commercial and political strength of the greater merchants, men such as Sir John Morden were to set the pattern of the eighteenth century. While men like the Barnardistons provided a link between the greater and lesser London merchants in the seventeenth century, leading the discontent of the lesser City elements against the Court, the late seventeenth- and early eighteenth-century years were to see an accentuation of these divisions with the fusion of the big financial and commercial City interest and the Whig aristocratic interest, a fusion that was to create the oligarchy upon which the political stability of the new century was to be built out of the chaos of the old.[11]

4

Sir John Morden

It is to his credit that he erected and endowed Morden College during his lifetime and lived to see the first members in residence.

John Evelyn, in his famous Diary records:

'9th June, 1695 Went afterwards to see Sir Jo. Morden's Charity or Hospital on Blackheath now building for the Reliefe of Merchants that have failed, a very worthy Charity & noble building.'

A facsimile of Sir John's signature

Morden College, Blackheath. From a work by J. Dalton, 1844.
This lithograph is 'Dedicated to the Trustees and Members by a Brother Member'.

In contrast to the principled opposition of some of the greater merchants in earlier years the political career of Sir John Morden was as typical of the new regime as it was short: in 1695 the tide of Eastern wealth swept him into the Whig representation of Colchester; in 1696 he lost his seat because of illegal electoral practices in the 1695 election.

In 1705 Sir John Morden valued his estates and other financial interests at some £34,000.[12] The value of his estates was set at £22,974, excluding his annual rental but for the rental of his fee-farm properties in Essex and Norfolk (the rental for these in 1711–12 was some £340 and in 1712–13 almost £280).[13] The 1707–8 rental of the Wricklemarsh estate was £215 (all figures hereafter are rounded up to the nearest pound), and that of the Old Court manor (1709–10) £624: these figures represented a return of 5 per cent and 6 per cent on the purchase prices, not including tithes in kind.[14] There is only scattered information on Morden's trading and commercial interests (insufficient to estimate their total value), though he was one of the original subscribers to the Bank of England (subscribing £4,000), and as late as 1707 he took shares in both ships and cargoes, his account books at this time showing a range of dealings from lead shares to bad debts.[15] The valuation of his 'trade' interests in 1705 at £4,679 of the £34,000 total almost certainly underestimates their true worth. Aside from the dealings in ships, cargoes and lead mining, these interests covered bank credits and shares in Bristol water works. Debts owed Sir John Morden were separately valued at £4,262 (many of them were 'desperate'), and his household goods at £1,426, just over £1,000 of which was made up of jewels and plate. The wide range of his investments was typical of the big London merchants of the time. At the time of his death, when the bulk of his income probably came from land, he was worth some £40,000 and enjoyed an annual income of something in excess of £1,500. If not among the foremost of the City merchant aristocrats Morden was still a very rich man.[16]

In seeking to perpetuate a family name the purchase of landed acres, the judicious marriage, and the installation of a son in county society was the almost invariable recourse of the big City merchants. For the Mordens, being childless, this road was barred. A short parliamentary career also circumscribed the possibility of present notability. In seeking an alternative the notable charitable foundations of the seventeenth century suggested themselves, and as early as 1693 Morden became a trustee of Bromley College in Kent, founded by the Bishop of Rochester for the widows of poor clergy and built in 1671. The decision to build Morden College seems to have been made about the early nineties, and the purchase of the leasehold of the manor of Old Court was made in 1698 as the principal endowment of the College. In 1699 Morden claimed that the building of the College had cost him £10,000 and that he was about to settle £1,000 as the annual cost of maintenance.[17] Thus did Sir John Morden set out to

Tombstone in memory of John Thompson, Yeoman of the Mouth to King Charles II, which is still preserved in the Old Burial Ground at the College. Thompson's College membership illustrates the links between the Crown and the greater merchants

match the enormous contemporary repute of Thomas Sutton's Charterhouse Hospital,[18] Guy's Hospital (founded on a lucky speculation in South Sea stock), and other large endowments of the day. The purpose of the college, in Morden's words to Daniel Defoe, was to enable merchants, '... as they had lived like gentlemen, they might die so'. Dying like a gentleman then meant having £40 per annum, lodging and diet, coals, a gown (for attending religious worship), and servants to look after the members' apartments. Dying was quickly to be made less comfortable than this generous provision allowed: Morden's failure to secure tax exemption for his charity meant that the allowance was cut from £40 to £15 during his years in authority over the College.

This authority was very much a personal, autocratic and paternalistic thing in the years before Morden's death in 1708. The College was essentially an extension of the Morden household: from his nearby mansion, acting as his own treasurer, using his own chaplain as the College Chaplain, Morden directed affairs with a minute attention to detail. The College was supplied from his estate, on which he ran his own dairy. As lay proprietor of most of the great tithes of Greenwich a tenth of agricultural produce came to him and thence to Morden College. The servants lived in at the College. Sir John obviously took pleasure as well as pains in reproducing the arrangements typical of a substantial country squire's patriarchal household.

In order to die like a gentleman it was necessary to live like a Christian, and the first regime of Morden College resembled most of those that followed in enjoining upon the members a strict and frequent adherence to the observances of the Church of England, as well as enforcing a rigorous attention to the demands of respectability and sobriety. The penalty for transgression of the major rules, immediate expulsion, was more severe than in similar contemporary institutions like Charterhouse. That the rules were not always obeyed, that autocracy was not borne lightly, and that the members were often neither respectable nor sober will be apparent as this work develops, and almost three centuries of College life are explored in detail. Before turning to this something more remains to be said about merchant society in London, and the role that charity had in reflecting and shaping this world. Morden was of a piece with the wealthy of his time: his will, in providing doles for the poor, and donations to hospitals, schools and imprisoned debtors, reflects the preoccupations of his fellow merchants.[19] It is to the ways in which philanthropy bodied forth these preoccupations that we shall first turn.

References for Chapter One

1. There are two printed histories of Morden College: Henry Lansdell, *Princess Aelfrida's Charity*, published in seven parts, Vol. I, pts 1–4 (1911), Vol. II, pts 5–7 (1914); T. Frank Green, *Morden College, Blackheath, Being the Tenth Monograph of the London Surrey Committee* (1916). Henry Lansdell was chaplain of Morden College, 1892–1912. His study, indispensable to any student of College affairs, was reprinted from articles in the Blackheath and area newspaper press.

2. For Sir John Morden's early life see H. Lansdell, *op. cit.*, Vol. I, pt 3, chap. XII; and for the best account of his subsequent career and the foundation of his College, *ibid.*, chaps. XIII–XXVI. Lansdell's account has been extensively drawn on for the purposes of this chapter. On Sir John Morden see also *Dictionary of National Biography*, esp. list of sources and citations given at end of biography.

3. On the Turkey Company see A. C. Wood, *A History of the Levant Company* (1935, reprinted 1964).

4. On the Brands cf. MSS account in Morden College Muniment Room compiled by Reginald Saw in 1966, 'The Lady Morden Story. Memoranda on the Brands of Edwardstone'; also H. Lansdell, *op. cit.*, chap. XII.

5. *DNB*; also H. Lansdell, *op. cit.*, chap. XV.

6. For the legend, 'rough notes' of Henry William Smith on Life of Sir John Morden and History of Morden College, Morden College Muniment Room. Smith was College Treasurer, 1819–72.

7. W. K. Jordan, *The Charities of London 1480–1660: The Aspirations and Achievements of the Urban Society* (1960), chap. V.

8. W. A. Speck, *Stability and Strife, England 1714–1760* (1977), pp. 73–4; see also G. Rude, *Hanoverian London, 1714–1808* (1971), pp. 54–6.

9. D. Defoe, *A Tour through the Whole Island of Great Britain* (first pub. 1724–6, ed. P. Rogers 1971), p. 114 (see also pp. 114–15 for a description of Morden College).

10. L. Stone, *The Causes of the English Revolution 1529–1642* (1972), pp. 55–6; J. H. Plumb, *The Growth of Political Stability in England, 1675–1725* (1967), pp. 24–6.

11. *Ibid.*, esp. pp. 184–6, and chap. I; J. H. Plumb, *Sir Robert Walpole, The Making of A Statesman* (1956), pp. 22–9.

12. Morden College Account Book, 1705–8 (Book 127, Muniment Room), 1705 General Account, dated 31 May 1705.

13. M.C. Account Book, 1708–68 (Book 89, Muniment Room).

14. On Sir John Morden's financial affairs see also H. Lansdell, *op. cit.*, chaps. XVII, XIX to XXI.

15. M.C. Account Books, 1705–8 (Books 127, 126, Muniment Room).

16. G. Rude, *op. cit.*, p. 56.

17. H. Lansdell, *op. cit.*, chap. XVII, p. 26.

18. N. R. Shipley, 'Full Hand and Worthy Purposes. The Foundation of Charterhouse, 1610–1616', *Guildhall Studies in London History*, Vol. 1, no. 4, April 1975.

19. Wills, inventories, etc. of Sir John and Lady Morden (Book 85), Morden College Muniment Room. By his will the use of Wricklemarsh House and its contents was left to Lady Morden, the rest of the estate directly endowing Morden College. Susan Morden was made sole executrix of the estate, and three trustees were appointed to run the College with her. Annuities were left to various relatives. £200 was provided for discharging bankrupts from debtors' prison, £100 to poor blind people, and small doles were given to the parochial poor. (The 1700 College Rule and Orders will also be found in Book 89.)

The Habit of a Merchant of
London about 1640

The Habit of a Wife of a Merchant
of London about 1640

CHAPTER TWO

Merchants Prosperous and Merchants Decayed: Charity and Genteel Poverty in London

By 1700 the gentry and the merchant class had for long achieved a position of dominance in the philanthropic life of the nation. Of the two, the mercantile interest, and especially the London merchants, were probably of overwhelming importance in stamping the character of their giving on the structure of seventeenth and eighteenth-century charity.[1] The characteristic instrument of merchant charity in the Tudor and Stuart period was the charitable trust. The institution of the trust marked the transition from the personal, often indiscriminate giving of alms to a more deliberate attention to the shaping of society. By the late seventeenth and early eighteenth centuries the decline of the clergy and nobility and the rise of the mercantile interest as charitable donors was expressed in the characteristics of charitable giving: merchants were men of business and their charity bore the marks of their preoccupations as men of business.

In mercantilist teaching the relationship of political economy and charity was such as to stress the need to preserve the labour force at sea, and the labour force at home (as the source of raw material manufacture). Increased population was understood to keep wages low and competition alive. Thus, if wages were to be kept low taxes were not to be oppressive, and charity was to act as a bounty to industry, regulating the balance between destitution and the prevention of idleness. In the terms of the time, 'it was prudent to relieve the wants of the poor but folly to remove them.' Much merchant charity at this time was therefore expressed in such institutions as the Marine Society and the Foundling Hospital (where boy entrants might be reared as seamen), dedicated as these were to the preservation of the nation's manpower and the fostering of the maritime interest.[2] Less specifically mercantile in character, the 'associated' charities of the late seventeenth and early eighteenth centuries represented an accentuation of commercial influence upon charitable giving. If the charitable trust marked a movement towards social intervention it still enshrined the wishes of the individual, setting his soul to rights before his Maker as well as his contemporaries. In such a man as Sir John Morden it expressed the particular way in which he desired to interpret and perpetuate his compassionate generosity. The 'associated' charity, on the other hand, seen particular in the Charity

School Movement, aggregated a more anonymous giving within a bureaucratic, institutionalised structure.[3]

The development of the joint stock company in the 1690's and the parallel growth in the associated charity was no accidental conjunction: the later seventeenth century years have justly been described in terms of a commercial and financial 'revolution'.[4] As foreign and internal trade penetrated further the fabric of the English economy, social institutions, among them charitable ones, took on the characteristics of economic institutions. At the same time a more calculating, less paternalist approach to social policy is apparent under the later Stuarts and early Hanoverians. Developments at the national level were reflected locally in the tightening-up of the Poor Law and a drying-up of the springs of private charity. Most revealing of all perhaps, between 1650 and 1750 charitable bequests to those outside the family of the donor diminished considerably.[5] After 1688 there was also a considerable decline in bequests to the London livery companies.[6] Thus the endowment of Morden College represented rather the latter days of an older and more compassionate tradition than the expression of more recent developments. The giving of men like Sir John Morden combined an understandable concern for the verdict of posterity with a genuine concern for his fellows: such altruism stood in sharp contrast to those in merchant society of equal wealth and standing who did not give. Of course the charitable trust continued to be of importance in the eighteenth century (and indeed thereafter), though the development of the 'associated' charity was to point to the future, and it is in its nineteenth century reflections that we shall consider it in due course.

Around the time of the foundation of Morden College a trading nation was often a nation at war in pursuit of the protection and advancement of trade. Not the least of the motives for charity at the time, and especially in merchant giving, was the assertion of nationalist, Protestant feeling against the spiritual and economic dangers of Catholic Europe. Defoe expressed the feelings of the nation in ending his fulsome praise for the charities of London on the following note:

'... so that the Papists have no reason to boast, that there were greater benefactions and acts of charity to the poor given in their time, than in our Protestant times ...'[7]

In the seventeenth century it has been estimated that the greater merchants contributed just under 60 per cent of the total of charitable wealth given by the City of London.[8] This degree of generosity continued in subsequent centuries, though as an expression of the influence and standing of the greater merchants it was of declining overall significance as the industry of the City outgrew its boundaries from the late eighteenth century onwards, and the reform movement of the nineteenth century began to bite (albeit very late and very incompletely)

12

into the privileges and powers of the Corporation and livery company charities.[9] Nonetheless, around the mid-nineteenth century, the dominance of the City of London in the structure of the nation's charity was still considerable, and the funds of the livery companies (from which much of merchant giving was drawn) were still immense.[10] Aside from the funds held by the companies themselves, many of their members acted as trustees for other charitable institutions, and the range of their giving extended from very big doles to the poor to education, hospitals and almshouses.[11]

Jordan's anatomy of merchant charity before 1660 provides a valuable means of interpreting London merchant society.[12] The greater merchants were the most worldly of all classes, giving only 13·52 per cent of their wealth for religious purposes. The poor received 40 per cent of donations directly, and 14 per cent of charitable wealth went for the purposes of 'rehabilitation': in this category loans to aspiring tradesmen and merchants amounted to more than half the amount given to hospitals. The interest of merchants in their own class was further reflected in charities to debtors (we have noted Sir John Morden's position in this respect), and to education (27·55 per cent of the total), in which the merchants' own cultural *milieu* benefited most in the form of the grammar schools (rather than the universities). Among the lesser merchants (some four-fifths of merchant donors), the poor received 42·57 per cent of the total, but education only 7·7 per cent, and religion 17·2 per cent. This brief outline of the relationship between charity and mercantile preoccupations serves to introduce more general questions concerning the relationship between charity and society.

Any attempt to explore the social psychology of the merchant community, and view the character of this community's social life in terms of its economic situation must be exploratory: despite their great significance in English life the London merchants from the seventeenth century onwards have received curiously little historical attention. Such an exploration might best begin with a consideration of the nature of mercantile wealth, unlike that of the landowner and manufacturer, something highly liquid, unfixed and disposable. Merchants were essentially speculators, and highly sensitive to the barometer of fortune. The natural difficulties of economic life were augmented by war, and the hazards of life in an overcrowded and unhygienic city (at least before the eighteenth century). The vicissitudes of merchant life are chronicled at length in the eighteenth-century novel, and reflected in the life and work of Daniel Defoe, as well as the list of bankruptcies in the *Gentleman's Magazine*.[13] In the first half of the century, in general a period of economic stability, the chronic instability that constantly underlay mercantile activity is reflected in the precariousness of London banking: in 1720 one-third of London's banks went under. There was thus what might be termed a natural impulse to charity as the instrument by which fortune was propitiated. The ease with which a fortune might be lost was equalled by the ease and speed with which one might be gained. In the eighteenth century the special character of merchant accumulation found expression in the profligacy of mercantile spending, a profligacy in contrast to the restraint of the other classes.[14] As Samuel Johnson was to put it,[15]

'... with what munificence a great merchant will spend his money ... whereas you will hardly find a country gentleman who is not a great deal disconcerted at an unexpected occasion to lay out pounds.'

The insecurity of mercantile wealth was directly reflected in merchant society: before 1660 the dynastic aspect of merchant commercial life was strikingly weak, between 1480 and 1660 (of those families considered by W. K. Jordan) no London merchant fortune passing through the third generation in the period.[16] The destination of such fortunes was invariably the landed estate. This situation was bound to change in the eighteenth century, after the seventeenth-century explosion in financial and commercial activity. The political reflection of this explosion, the fusion of the big commercial interests and aristocratic landed society to effect the oligarchy upon which the eighteenth-century whig ascendancy was based, meant that the aspiration to gentry standing might be greatly qualified by the pride and self-confidence of a merchant elite. And, indeed, compared to the preceding century, the eighteenth century does seem to have been a period of improved status for merchants.[17] Nor, of course, was there ever an inevitable transfer into landed status. Land might be bought as a means of independent income only, and, where a landed seat was set up, this by no means meant a severance from urban and commercial life. Sir John Morden himself, and the families he married into, illustrate this sort of landed involvement, as does the practice of Hull and Leeds merchants in the eighteenth century.[18] Similarly, there had always been a high degree of social and economic interaction between land and business: merchants speculated in land, the landed interest practised many of the mercantile virtues in the economic exploitation of its lands, and the sons of the gentry and aristocracy were sometimes apprenticed to merchant houses, especially those connected with the great chartered companies.

Thus, there was no simple progression to landed status, and the degree of dynastic continuity in commerce in the eighteenth century was considerable, among the Glasgow tobacco lords as among the Hull and Leeds merchants.[19] Though the eighteenth century probably saw an increase in merchant self-esteem and a sharper accent on the inherited family business (as compared with previous centuries) London merchants were not provincial merchants. Unlike the rootedness of provincial mercantile cultures, and their easy and self-confident commerce with landed society, the more complex and varied economic and social organisation of London no doubt led to a weaker hereditary commit-

14

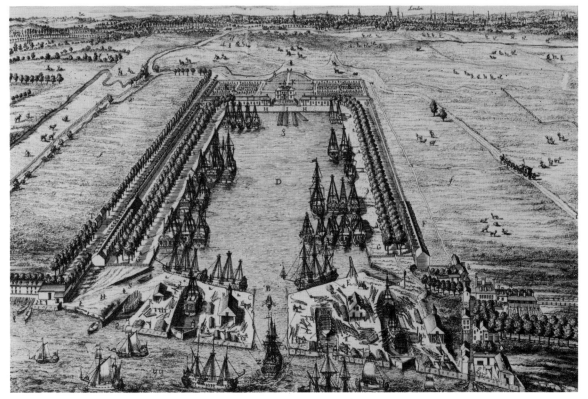

Howland Great Dock at Rotherhithe, near Deptford, capable of taking 120 Merchant ships and was much used by vessels of the East India Company during the lifetime of John Morden

ment to the merchant house. The spoils and diversions were greater, as were the dangers of failure. Even in the eighteenth century the tendency to perpetuate the remembrance of the family name rather than the family business was strong,[20] and this was probably more marked in London. Especially in comparison with landed and manufacturing society, primogeniture was unusual, capital tending to be split between trade and land with the emphasis in the end very much on perpetuating the landed side. Landed status in the eighteenth century, and for long after, continued to be of predominant worth in English social and political life.[21] To Dr. Johnson, merchants in the eighteenth century were still 'a new species of gentlemen'.[22]

Thus the nature of merchant society, especially in London, and the character of merchant wealth meant that land and charity were perhaps the two chief means of perpetuating a family name and reputation. Sir John Morden's purchase of an old gentry seat in Blackheath near to the social round of the Court, and his regime at Morden College – playing the country squire down to the last paternalist detail in both College and estate – nicely sums up in its fusion of landed status and charitable concern the areas in which the search for social standing was most completely concentrated. Charity, however, had many different functions in mercantile society.

15

It may have been of particular significance in reflecting and shaping the pecking order within the merchant community. It was only around 1600 that the distinction between merchants, involved in trans-maritime trade, and 'tradesmen', wholesalers and dealers in the inland trade, became clearly marked.[23] The requirements for entry into Morden College, considered in detail later, were emphatic in their exclusion of tradesmen and retailers. Across this line of demarcation was scored another and more emphatic one, that separating the great from the lesser in the merchant community as a whole. Estimates of the structure of London merchant society around the middle of the eighteenth century suggest that around 1000 of 10–15,000 merchants and principal tradesmen could be classified as large.[24] Among these was certainly John Morden, and the trustees who followed him were similarly drawn from the cream of London commercial and financial life. Though the College records do not enable us to tell, it is probable that the undercurrent of conflict between great and lesser played a considerable part in the high degree of disharmony that marked College life.

It was in fact around Morden's time that the large merchants and 'monied' interest – jointly represented in the great chartered companies, the Bank of England, and the two leading insurance corporations – fused to dominate the commercial life of the City, exert enormous pressure on government, and excite the bitter opposition of the lesser merchants, tradesmen and master craftsmen who made up the City freemen and much of the livery companies. This conflict of the *magnati* and *popolani* was to be played out in terms of the City and the Corporation in the form of the Court of Aldermen against the Court of Common Council.[25] It was to be a constant theme in the eighteenth century finding direct reflection in the social composition of the Wilkite and anti-Wilkite forces in 1769.[26] The trustees of Morden College in the eighteenth and nineteenth century were drawn from the institutional constellation that represented the City elite, and though the membership of the College included those who were once fairly eminent in merchant life (so that the *magnati-popolani* correspondence is not quite exact), there were more than sufficient of the lesser sort of merchant to make it likely that the history of the College cannot be altogether divorced from the long and bitter struggle between City and Corporation, vested interest and 'democracy'. Though conflict in the nineteenth century was less visible and political it no doubt continued underground in the form of manners, anxieties and resentments. The history of other City institutions in the eighteenth and nineteenth centuries similarly discloses a history of manifest and latent conflict. St. Bartholomew's Hospital, for instance, was the source of conflict between the vested interest of its governors (among whom were many of the City elite) and the 'democratic' forces in the Corporation.[27]

The pleasures of giving in the eighteenth century were certainly sharpened by

16

prevailing mental climate. The Enlightenment emphasis on the improvability of mankind was expressed in eighteenth-century Humanitarianism, with its delight in the rational emotion and the tender sensation of pity.[28] Behind this often superficial manifestation vital, Evangelical religion increasingly fostered the letter, if not always the spirit, of charity as the century wore on. And behind tender sensations and vital religion one discerns from time to time a current of asceticism and piety that recalls vanished structures of feeling. Thomas Cooke, Bank of England director, Turkey Company merchant and Morden College trustee, is a case in point. Cooke was borne to his grave by twelve poor housekeepers of the Newington (savings) box club with which he was associated in life. He was to be buried in a blanket, after the fashion of the Eastern winding sheet, and his common coffin was to be left to Morden College for the first corpse it would fit.[29] Sir John Morden, worldly-wise as he was, asked to be carried to his grave 'without any pomp and singing Boys but decently', a modesty which again highlights the complexity of motive behind charitable giving, the impossibility of reducing charitable acts purely and simply to acts of social authority and patronage. However, as suggested in the previous remarks on early eighteenth-century state policy and the diminution of bequests, endowments, and personal giving, this austerity was to wither in the course of the century.

Bernard Mandeville's contention, in the *Fable of the Bees* published in 1723, that Pride and Vanity built more Hospitals than all the Virtues together would seem nearer the mark. In the same years, the praise which Defoe lavished upon Thomas Sutton's Charterhouse ('the greatest noblest gift that ever was given for charity, by any man, public or private, in this nation, since history gives us account of things'), and the attention with which he catalogued the great charitable foundations and donors of the day, make it clear that the donor's claim upon posterity was staked with some effect before a receptive public at the time.[30] A century later, Lord Hobhouse, a leading figure in the parliamentary reform of charity, displayed a scepticism as salutary as Mandeville's in remarking upon the motives of pious founders,[31]

> '. . . he thinks himself ill-used when he finds he cannot regulate the affairs of two or three unborn generations. It is needless to say how warmly a man of his mental attitude may embrace the notion of extending his domain by giving his property to public uses for ever. The passions akin to love of power are ostentatiousness, which is gratified by the perpetuation of one's own name and money, and vanity, which induces a man to think that he can judge better what Society is likely to want, than Society itself does.'

Behind the tender sensation of pity in eighteenth century-Humanitarianism lurked the pleasures of visiting the lowly. In the nineteenth century 'slumming' was to become a major pastime of the rich, especially the idle portion of it, and especially among women.[32] And, if the dignity of Thomas Cooke's passing was real enough and his contact with the poor direct and personal, then it was no less true that this kind of death and this kind of charity were very often a reflection of considerations arising more from the marketplace than from the moral conscience. Cooke's twelve pallbearers were to be paid in alms, clothes and drink for the day. Recourse to paying the poor to attend funerals was common in the eighteenth century: an aristrocrat might pay 5/- in money and 40/- in clothes to each of 250 poor who went to his grave, or an octogenerian woman pay poor, old women to attend her funeral.[33] The poor were alive to the possibilities of gain, and the relationship entered into, whatever the pretensions of the donor, was very often merely contractual. Respectable donors' outrage at the rapacity of the poor is a commonplace in the history of charity and patronage. Yet the respectable classes fallen from grace were as prone as the poor to take a mercenary attitude to what was on offer. There is in fact considerable value in treating the history of charity as a branch of business history.

The charity brief in the eighteenth century is a case of charity being run explicitly on business lines. Organised by groups of people needing relief, usually as a consequence of some community disaster, appeal by the charity brief involved a complex chain of organisation that stretched from the trustees and 'undertakers' who sent out the briefs, the officials who received them in the parishes to which they were sent, to the Lord Chancellor, His Majesty's Proctors, and the Registrar of the Court of Chancery. All received due and not inconsiderable award for their efforts.[34] If the solicitations of the genteel poor did not take this institutional form there was a distinct ring of the marketplace to them: the gentle poor advertised in the press, which put the solicitous in contact with the donors, and subsequently published details of the latter's generosity (the needy were often at pains to say grateful acknowledgement would be made). The tavern and the coffee house acted as a kind of charity exchange, in which letters of reference were lodged and the needy sometimes viewed by their prospective patrons.[35] The gentle poor had of course a degree of access to the funds and connections putting them in touch with this highly organised activity that was lacking among the working poor.

Yet both the gentle and working poor stood in a similar relation to the donor of charity, one of dependence and thus potential subordination. What is so interesting about charity then, and what has been so little studied in the writing of its history, is the insight it gives us into the vast range of such situations of subordination in society, and people's acceptance of them and their resistance to them. In interpreting such situations within groups and classes the history of institutions like Morden College is especially useful. For the donor what the gift so often conferred was power. The degree of power might be limited or non-

18

Thames side – the homecoming of the merchant fleet – view of the Custom House Wharf,
1757. The first and second buildings were destroyed by fire. The third, designed by Wren
and completed about 1671 was damaged by fire in 1718 and later reconstructed by
Thomas Ripley

existent where giving was corporate or anonymous, but, as we shall see, so much
of eighteenth- and nineteenth-century giving brought with it influence and
control over the actual dispensation of the gift. When charity was centred upon a
fairly closed world – such as a factory, an estate, a neighbourhood, or an institution like Morden College – the potential for acquiring power and influence
might be immense.

Of course, giving brought other things than power; and benefits that might be
just as valuable to the donor. As we have seen, it brought the chance to display
his wealth and improve his social standing. It could also bring him the contacts
that helped him to prosperity and influence in other spheres. As we shall see in
the next chapter, the Morden College trustees were enabled by their involvement in the finances of the College to diversify their knowledge and contacts
into other spheres of business life. Trustee involvement in institutions like the
College also served to bind the City commercial elite even more firmly together,
especially in view of the often familial nature of this involvement. For the less
exalted in society – as a mirror-image of the joys of 'slumming' – a charitable
donation might bring the chance to move in the world of the rich and the well-
connected. The charitable society of the nineteenth century, with its social whirl
of bazaars, balls, *soirees* and *conversaziones*, brought rewards and pleasures in this
world more useful and pressing than those to be gained in the next, especially
when the mingling was done in the marbled halls of the great London charity
headquarters.[36] Important as these considerations are, however, it is rather the
relation of patronage and influence to charity that will be approached here.
Thus in the history of the College, the relationship between the trustees, the
administrative hierarchy of the College (including the servants), and the
members will be the theme that most often detains us.

19

The operation of charity as power and as business can be best illuminated by the mechanics of patronage. The degree to which the charity world in the eighteenth and nineteenth centuries can be understood as a highly intricate network of patrons and client-candidates has largely been lost to view, and throws light on little-considered aspects of the history of philanthropy. This is because the extent to which the charitable subscription openly bought the right to preferment has not been fully understood. In the mid-nineteenth century admission to a number of the five Royal Hospitals, for instance, was by the recommendation of subscribers and governors who bought the right to nominate with their donation. This right was established on a business-like, *pro-rata* basis at some places: at the Westminster Hospital subscribers could recommend one in-patient and two out-patients for every annual guinea given or £10 donated. Subscriptions at the more exalted level of governorships could also buy places on the Management Committees of hospitals and many other charities.[37] For the poor, admission into orphanages or apprenticeships might be by the letter of recommendation of influential subscribers and patrons. A benefit received in youth might involve a connection, and thus an element of dependence, that continued through life. A young man helped to an apprenticeship by the City Guilds or the Provident Societies could expect a degree of continuing help in his later career.[38] It is clear that the implied understanding on which donations were forthcoming was often that the subscriber should have a say in who should be selected for benefit.[39]

This was especially the case with the Benevolent Pension and Benefit Societies of the mid-nineteenth century, which represented probably the chief recourse of the gentle poor. Candidates for support from the principal Pension Society, the National Benevolent Institution founded in 1812, had to be supported by a clergyman and eight subscribers (four of whom had to be householders). Annual election was by the vote of life-governors and subscribers, the franchise for whom was again established on a pecuniary *pro-rata* basis (200 guineas down gave the right to nominate a pensioner at once!). It is clear that considerable politicking went on at these elections when votes were loaned, petitioned and no doubt sometimes bought. The British Beneficent Society was set up in 1850 to correct the worse features of the old method of election. Canvassing and loaning were to be attacked by the ballot of the directors acting on the advice of the subscribers. But, as a contemporary handbook of London charities remarked, '... we must doubt whether the old plan pursued by the N.B.I. will not continue the favourite with the public, securing the power as it does, of electing the candidates in the hands of the subscribers.'[40] A number of the smaller Pension Societies permitted the votes for a candidate given at one election to be carried over to subsequent years so that a man 'with few friends' might have the chance of election.

20

This brief glimpse into what can fairly be termed the underworld of charity suggests not only the extent of patronage but something of its operation. Of this world we still know little, and it is questions rather than answers that most readily suggest themselves: were particular sectors of philanthropy tied together by the interest of key, strategically-placed patrons? and, if they were, can we imagine some system of patronage-broking and organised intelligence? We know little about the connections between patronage and particular churches and congregations, between business houses, workplaces and charity, and nothing at all about the social history of the letter of recommendation (a possible market in such 'recommends', their rhetorical form, and the form of petitions).

Patronage in English life has been so often viewed in political terms that the extent of social patronage is not always appreciated. A recognition of its true place prompts some qualification of the broad truth that the eighteenth century witnessed a diminution in personal and direct giving and the rise of corporate, relatively anonymous charity (a development seen in the post 1700 growth of 'associated' charity). Charity construed as a species of patronage indeed involved the operation of personal knowledge, and a degree of personal contact, though charity was nonetheless organised on increasingly institutional and bureaucratic lines, and this goes for most of the nineteenth-century bodies in which patronage obtained. Also, as already suggested, there could be a great deal of anonymity and indirection about the operation of charity in this way, as patron contacted patron above the head of the importuning candidate. The second, and major qualification to the notion of increasing anonymity cannot be pursued here. As argued elsewhere,[41] the paternalism of the northern factory masters in the second half of the nineteenth century can be seen, in the ostensibly unlikely sphere of industrial capitalism, to mark a recrudescence of the personal in charitable provision, though here the social force of paternalism – immense as it was – was qualified by prevailing middle-class notions of economic and social philosophy and the creation of a working-class tradition in the crucible of industrialisation. However, though it might have paternalist over-tones, most of the charity considered here under the heading of patronage was at a considerable remove from industrial paternalism, paternalism itself perhaps best being understood in the context of economic organisation, whether the unit of that organisation be the household, the estate or the factory.[42]

The poverty of the formerly better-off, termed here the gentle or genteel poor, is a subject perhaps even less considered than patronage in charity. The fact that we lack a descriptive terminology for this section of the poor is indication enough of this neglect. As with patronage, only the most general and speculative remarks can be made here on the question, though the history of Morden College will in course illuminate many aspects of both topics. In the mid-nineteenth century perhaps the two chief areas of provision for the genteel poor were the recently formed Pension and Benefit Societies, and the asylums and almshouses for the aged poor. Aside from these two chief areas there were many other institutions, including societies for the relief of debtors, and numerous endowments and gifts outside the immediate sphere of the aged. The City livery companies were the chief source of these (especially the Twelve Great Companies), and provision included help for members' widows and orphans, for debtors and apprentices, and the provision of scholarships and exhibitions to the children of liverymen and freemen, and even (in the Drapers Company), marriage portions for members donating to Company funds.[43] Because the livery companies most often directed charity outside their own institutions (though this was in many of its modern aspects a consequence of the late nineteenth-century pressure of reform), the degree to which they acted as self-help institutions for their members should not be forgotten. This function was inseparable from the corporate ritual of meetings, dinners, and elections, by which a good deal of the business and political life of the City was organised.[44] Charity thus complemented fellowship in the companies, and both go far to account for the strikingly integrated and coherent character of City economic and political life in the nineteenth century.

The much more recent growth of the Pension and Benefit Societies is of particular interest. The line separating each sort of institution is difficult to draw, the Benefit Societies, like the Pension, relying on voluntary contributions but being chiefly supported by pensioners' own contributions.[45] All of these societies active in 1850 had been founded since 1812. The simultaneous rise to prominence of middle-class beside working-class institutions of self-help (co-ops, friendly societies, benefit societies) is a conjunction of considerable historical interest. Part of the reason for the growth of the middle-class societies was a decline in funds, especially endowment funds, to homes for the aged. This development is in turn to be attributed to the implementation of the New Poor Law after 1834, the spread of the workhouse and the increase in the poor rate. It is also to be attributed to what a contemporary termed the modern realisation of charity as 'active consideration and judgement united with personal exertions.'[46] This realisation was itself a reflection of the mid-Victorian emphasis on the reconstitution of the community of the classes, a community sense believed shattered by the growth of population and industry in the nineteenth century. The visiting society, above all the Charity Organisation Society later in the century, was the characteristic instrument of this wish. It was a wish as illusory as the myth of the lost golden age of paternalist community. The realities of London were the inescapable ones of poverty and of class, in the mind of the visitor as of the visited.[47]

Perhaps a more pressing reason for the growth of Pension and Benefit Societies was in fact the wish to save the formerly well-off from the rigours of a

The Royal Exchange (second building). After the destruction of Gresham's original building in the Great Fire of 1666, a new and considerably larger building designed by Edward Jerman was erected. This was also destroyed by fire in 1838

Poor Law against which the working poor in London often had little defence. The most obvious (and the most revealing) thing about provision for the gentle poor was that it made their poverty easier to bear than the poverty of the working poor: in poverty as in wealth two worlds were maintained in distinction and separation. As the history of Morden College will make clear, the desire of the respectable donor and recipient to maintain station by maintaining a high degree of exclusiveness was reflected in the actual provision made for the gentle poor. As important as better food and clothes and the provision of servants were in fact the barriers erected around them. The city company almshouses were usually restricted to members, and requirements based on residence and character as well as occupation were often made. Eligibility for the Pension and Benefit Societies was often made dependent on a candidate not receiving parochial relief (in some cases *never* having received such relief). Independence and station were to be available in the Societies more than in any other institution: the National Benevolent Institution provided pensions for 'gentry, merchants, tutors, governesses' and those in the professional pursuits and the higher departments of trade. The British Beneficent Society catered for, among others, 'widows and unmarried daughters of persons who have moved in superior stations in society'. While the Pension Societies recruited from the genteel poor at large, the Benefit Societies worked among individual avocations. In the London of 1850 there were over seventy of these, catering for people as different as clergymen, naval and military officers, merchants, doctors, lawyers, old Etonians, printers, dancers and pawnbrokers. Those on the borderline

23

between gentlefolk and the poor were given special attention, representing as they did the frontier between classes, an area that had to be patrolled with constant vigilance. In the eighteenth century the borderland of housekeepers and tradesmen was the object of special interest,[48] and at all times the retainers of the notable (governesses, old servants, tutors) were given special attention.

Turning from the Societies to homes for the better-off aged, Morden College can assuredly be ranked among the 'superior' of such institutions (the inferior-superior distinction was made by Sampson Low junior, in 1850).[49] These asylums and almshouses, most of which were founded before 1700, represent the traditional face of charity; the Societies, continuing the emphasis on 'associated charity', the new. The most important group within the 'superior' designation were the better City company homes, known, as all such elevated institutions, as colleges or hospitals. Right of nomination might be shared with the London parishes and other bodies, as was the case with Sion College, Aldermanbury, and Queen Elizabeth College, in Greenwich. Whittington's College in Highgate provided for those of 'chaste and good conversation', and the most famous college of all, Charterhouse (not a company institution) similarly expressed the exclusiveness that accounted for the 'superior' reputation – those having experienced 'better days' were preferred.

The lustre of Charterhouse was expressed in its association with royalty. The governors were also made up of the leading aristocratic lights of the day. The advantages of being a college rather than an almshouse member were expressed in pecuniary terms – allowances and provision were superior, and nowhere more superior than at Morden College itself. The clergy and dependents were catered for at St. Katherine's Hospital and Bromley College, and enjoyed the support of a whole galaxy of institutions apart from these. At St. Katherine's the Master enjoyed a 'handsome villa and pleasure ground'. Only partly qualifying under the heading of genteel poverty, were the two Royal Hospitals at Greenwich and Chelsea, for superannuated seamen and soldiers, respectively: in 1850 the latter provided 539 in-pensions to members, and 70,000 out-pensions; the former 2710 in-pensions and between 13–14,000 out-pensions. Many of the lesser almshouses were in the gift of the City companies also – the Fishmongers ran 94 of these throughout the country. These also catered for decayed housekeepers and ratepayers, and sometimes the parish poor. The East India Company had its own almshouse, catering for the widows of petty officers and captains (the pension of the latter was graded according to the rank of the husband). The Freemasons had their own almshouse (and a number of Societies), but the most impressive of these lesser bodies was the Licensed Victuallers' Asylum in the Old Kent Road. Instituted in 1827 and incorporated in 1842 the Asylum represents rather the recent development of occupational self-help among the better-off, than the old world to which Morden College belonged.

24

Before considering the daily regime of the College in detail something more remains to be said about the *experience* of receiving charity. Charitable patronage has been seen to have established the potential for power and influence, but it is the realisation of this power among the dependent, in terms of acquiescence and resistance, that poses the really interesting questions of interpretation. Charity was invariably used as a means of moral reformation. Of course, it was usually the working poor that stood most in need of reformation in the minds of the governors. Distinguishing the 'deserving' from the 'undeserving' poor, 'setting the poor on work', and encouraging the virtues of thrift and sobriety among the deserving were aims that characterised private charity and public policy down the ages. The tendency to regard the poor as congenitally if not irremediably sunk in the error of its ways is indeed not completely absent in the present. It is a tendency that has been well chronicled by historians. What has been less investigated is the moralistic use of charity toward the rich fallen from their station, and it is this that the history of Morden College so much illuminates.

For, if the moral stigma that the wealthy so often imputed to the poor was not present (or at least pronounced), then the stigma of failure certainly was. What is especially interesting about College life is the authoritarian rigour with which respectability and religion were enjoined upon an often unhappy and unwilling membership. But what the College authorities and trustees attempted in the eighteenth and nineteenth centuries, before the development of a more liberal and generous attitude around 1900, was less the reformation of character than the maintenance of those moral virtues that marked out the gentleman from his inferiors. Understanding the interplay of acceptance and resistance in situations of dependence is a complex matter that cannot be fully entered into here.[50] In situations where the world of the dependent is a fairly closed and inward-looking one in which the patron is an integral and essential part (and in which the experience of dependence is everywhere apparent), the capacity for acquiescence and a more positive acceptance of the moral order of the institution is very often realised at its fullest. The institution may be a factory, an estate, a household or – in a particularly extreme form – a closed and 'total' institution like Morden College.

The experience of failure is in fact central to an understanding of how the moral authority of an institution like Morden College was secured. For many of the College members the days of poverty had meant a harsh exposure to the daily reality of life among the mass of the labouring poor. In seeking to implement the moral order that marked out the gentleman from his inferiors, and so gave expression to the physical privileges of existence in the College, this awareness of the depths below was crucial. Perhaps more than any other pressure acting upon the members it served to harmonise the purpose of the College authorities and the behaviour of the members.

As the East India Company grew in strength it built and launched its own ships. This reproduction shows the launch of the East Indiaman *Edinburgh* from the Blackwall yard of Messrs Wigrams and Green on November 9th, 1825

(Courtesy of Port of London Authority. From a print in the Authority's Collection)

In Morden College – where the members were usually completely destitute and dependent on the College – it is clear that the members, more often than not, acquiesced in the moral regime of the College as the means by which something of their station and respectability could be retrieved and maintained until death. If in places like Morden College the capacity for scepticism and opposition was limited by dependence, and by the *esprit de corps* engendered in such 'total' institutions, then this is only part of the story. There is perhaps no greater danger than that of interpreting relations of dependence and hierarchic subordination in society in the simple terms of a unilateral imposition of authority upon an unresisting and inert object. As Edward Thompson has seen, such relations are invariably to be considered as a relationship, in which domination is secured only by exercising constraint on both parties.[51] What are involved are *reciprocal* rights and obligations, boundaries that define the limits of opposition at the same time as they give that opposition a pretext and a form. And charity is to be construed in these terms also, as is, in a particularly helpful manner, the history of single institutions.

The ethos of Morden College was defined not only by the regime of its authorities but also by the experience the members brought with them from the world outside. They brought with them their own notions of what a gentleman should feel and do, and how he should therefore be treated; and when those in . authority acted in accordance with these feelings the world of Morden College tended to be a placid one. When these expectations were not met, when reciprocity was spurned, the result was often conflict and discord. The earlier history of the College is thus in part the history of sensitivity to the condescension usually implicit, and often explicit, in those holding the reins of power and patronage in College life. As we have seen, it was a sensitivity compounded by social conflict within the merchant community itself, between the greater and their economic and social inferiors. The element of conflict in College life was also fed by what can be termed the natural anarchy of the aged, a desire to throw off restraint and inhibition in the last years of life. This seems often to have been in tension with the desire for order, quiet and obedience that marked a standing lost and at last retrieved.

Though the history of the College will be told in narrative form these are the themes that will inform the treatment of events, for it is only in attempting to recapture the recipients' experience of charity that the role of charity in society can be fully understood. However, something of the detail of College estate management must first be considered, for if the primary interest of College history lies in the relations of members and authorities, these relations are also illuminated by the finances of the estate. The College was a considerable landlord and a major force in shaping the development of an important part of London.

References for Chapter Two

1. W. K. Jordan, *Philanthropy in England 1480–1660: A Study of the Changing Patterns of English Social Aspirations* (1959), chap. I.

2. D. Owen, *English Philanthropy 1660–1960* (1965), pp. 14–15; W. S. Lewis and R. W. Williams, *Private Charity in England 1747–1757* (1938), a useful book of texts and not-so-useful linking commentary.

3. D. Owen, *op. cit.*, Pt. I, intro. and chap. 3.

4. P. G. M. Dickson, *The Financial Revolution in England. A Study of the Development of Public Credit 1688–1756* (1967); W. E. Minchinton (ed.), *The Growth of English Overseas Trade in the Seventeenth and Eighteenth Centuries* (1969).

5. W. A. Speck, *Stability and Strife in England 1714–1760* (1977), pp. 78–9.

6. W. F. Kahl, 'The development of the London Livery Companies', publication no. 15, Kress Library of Business and Economics, Baker Library, Harvard University (1960). However, the early eighteenth century was something of an Indian Summer for endowments and bequests, cf. D. Owen, *op. cit.* pp. 73–4.

7. D. Defoe, *A Tour Through the Whole Island of Great Britain* (first published 1724–6, ed. P. Rogers, 1971), p. 334.

8. W. K. Jordan, *The Charities of London: The Aspirations and Achievements of the Urban Society* (1960), chap. V.

9. W. F. Kahl, *loc. cit.*, D. Owen, *op. cit.*, chap. X.

10. D. Owen, *op. cit.*, pp. 191–3.

11. E. Lascelles, 'Charity' in G. M. Young (ed.), *Early Victorian England 1830–1865* (1934), Vol. II. On the importance of the greater mercantile-commercial interest in London charity in the eighteenth century, and on the City companies, D. Defoe, *op. cit.*, pp. 329–34, the best single guide to the structure of charitable provision in eighteenth-century London.

12. W. K. Jordan, *op. cit.*, chap. V.

13. W. A. Speck, *op. cit.*, pp. 75–6. For an interesting background work see C. P. Kindleberger, *Manias, Panics and Crashes: A History of Financial Crises* (1978).

14. W. E. Minchinton, 'The Merchants in England in the Eighteenth Century', *Explorations in Entrepreneurial History*, X, December 1957, No. 2 (Harvard University), p. 69.

15. *Ibid.*

16. W. K. Jordan, *Charities of London*, chap. V, also *Philanthropy in England*, chap. VII, sect. C.

17. W. A. Speck, *op. cit.*, pp. 73–4; see also, on the standing of merchants, R. B. Westerfield, 'Middlemen in English Business, Particularly Between 1660 and 1760', *Transactions of the Connecticut Academy of Arts and Sciences*, Vol. 19, pp. 111–445, May 1915, (Yale U.P., 1915), pp. 403–4. Westerfield's work is an invaluable guide to the techniques of the market, and the economic and social structure of English commercial life.

18. G. Jackson, *Hull in the Eighteenth Century: A Study in Economic and Social History* (Oxford 1972), chaps. V, XI; R. G. Wilson, *Gentlemen Merchants: the merchant community in Leeds, 1700–1830* (Manchester 1971).

19. T. M. Devine, *The Tobacco Lords: A Study of the Tobacco Merchants of Glasgow, c. 1740–1790* (Edinburgh 1975), chaps. 1, 2, 3, 6.

20. W. E. Minchinton, *loc. cit.*, p. 69.

21. See D. Marshall's discussion of social structure and social mores, *English People in the Eighteenth Century* (1956), chap. 2.

22. Quoted in R. B. Westerfield, *op. cit.* p. 403.

23. R. B. Westerfield, *op. cit.*, pp. 330–1. See also Anon, *A General Description of All Trades* ... (1747), p. 140, and R. Campbell, *The London Tradesmen* (1747), David and Charles reprint 1969.

24. G. Rude, *Hanoverian London 1714–1808* (1971), p. 53. The simple division between greater and lesser will suffice for present purposes, but on the 'middling' sort of merchant, see J. H. Plumb, *Sir Robert Walpole* (1956), pp. 27–9.

25. L. Sutherland, 'The City of London in Eighteenth Century Politics', in R. Pares and A. J. Taylor (eds.), *Essays Presented to Sir Lewis Namier*, (1956). On London merchants and merchant houses see R. Pares' essay in the same volume, also L. B. Namier, 'Anthony Bacon M.P. An Eighteenth Century Merchant', *Jnl. of Economic and Business History*, Vol. II, No. 1, November 1929.

26. G. Rude, 'The Anti-Wilkite Merchants of 1769', *The Guildhall Miscellany*, Vol. II, No. 7, September 1975.

27. N. J. M. Kerling, 'The Relations between St. Bartholemew's Hospital and the City of London, 1546–1948', *The Guildhall Miscellany*, Vol. IV, No. 1, October 1971.

28. D. Owen, *op. cit.*, Pt. I, chaps. 1 and 2.

29. W. S. Lewis and R. W. Williams, *op. cit.*, chap. 6.

30. D. Defoe, *op. cit.*, p. 334, see also pp. 329–334. Thomas Sutton (1532–1611) was a Durham coal entrepreneur who left £130,000 to charity. For Mandeville see 'An Essay on Charity and Charity Schools' (1723) in B. Mandeville, *The Fable of the Bees* (Penguin 1970).

31. Quoted in E. Lascelles, *loc. cit.*, p. 345.

32. See Brian Harrison's review of D. Owen's book, 'Philanthropy and the Victorians', *Victorian Studies*, Vol. IX, No. 4, June 1966.

33. Lewis and Williams, *op. cit.*, chap. 6.

34. *Ibid.*

35. *Ibid.*, chap. 5.

36. D. Owen, *op. cit.*, Pt. II, chaps. IV, VI; B. Harrison, *loc. cit.*

37. S. Low, jun., *The Charities of London* (1850), chap. I.

38. E. Lascelles, *loc. cit.*, pp. 323–4.

39. *Ibid.*, pp. 324–7.

40. S. Low, *op. cit.*, p. 242; this paragraph is based on S. Low, chaps. XII, XIII; see also chap. VII.

41. P. Joyce, *Work, Society and Politics: The Culture of the Factory in Later Victorian England* (Harvester Press and Rutgers University Press, 1980).

42. The historical and sociological distinction between charity, patronage and paternalism cannot be considered here. A useful discussion is N. Abercrombie and S. Hill, 'Paternalism and patronage', *British Journal of Sociology*, XXVII, No. 4, Dec. 1976. The whole question of patronage and charity will be treated by me at a later date, in one or more scholarly articles, in part arising from the present work on Morden College.

43. S. Low, *op. cit.*, chap. X. On London charities in general see also the less useful, A. Highmore, *Pietas Londinensis* (1810).

44. W. F. Kahl, *loc. cit.*; see also the very interesting W. Purdie Treloar, *A Lord Mayor's Diary 1906–7* (1920).

45. On these Societies see S. Low, *op. cit.*, chaps. XII, XIII; also E. Lascelles, *loc. cit.*, pp. 326–7.

46. *Ibid.*, chap. XI, intro.

47. G. Stedman Jones, *Outcast London: A Study in the relationship between classes in Victorian Society* (Oxford 1971).

48. W. S. Lewis and R. W. Williams, *op. cit.*, chap. V.

49. S. Low, *op. cit.*, chap. XI.

50. See my discussion in P. Joyce, *op. cit.*, chap. 3.

51. See esp. E. P. Thompson, 'Eighteenth-Century English Society: class struggle without class?', *Social History*, Vol. 3, No. 2, May 1978.

Sundial set up by the Trustees in 1725
'for keeping the clock right which often goes wrong'

CHAPTER THREE

Estate and College
Finance and Management

The basis of the College income in the eighteenth century, and for long after the chief source of its financial support, was the Blackheath and Greenwich lands with which Sir John Morden endowed his creation. Land and property rentals, sales, and purchases have assured the College a steady and growing income from the date of its foundation. Thus the history of the College is not only an aspect of the history of charity and the history of the decayed rich but in its economic aspect also throws light on the history of landownership and estate management in England.

The annual rental of the Wricklemarsh and Old Court properties[1] received in Morden's day was maintained at much the same level until the sale of the former in 1723 after Dame Susan Morden's death. The purchaser was Sir Gregory Page, son of a Wapping brewer who had made a pile out of the South Sea Bubble. Of the £9,000 received from the sale £8,000 went into South Sea annuities until suitable investments in land could be made. Investments in the dividend market such as this characterised the whole history of the College, but the preference for investment in land and property expressed in 1723 was to be the chief feature of estate management thereafter. After the sale of Wricklemarsh the emphasis was to be on the husbanding of the landed estate rather than its lucrative disposal.

The total annual income of the College in the eighteenth century continued around £1,700 until the 1780s when, between 1779–80 and 1789–90, it increased from £1,701 to £2,786 (all figures rounded up to the nearest pound here and hereafter). It continued around this level until the second great period of growth in the 1820s and 30s.[2] In the eighteenth century a small proportion of College income came from bank annuities, and such investments of Morden's as waterworks and lead mining (the latter seem to have been disposed of fairly early in the century). Consols and government stocks were a more important source of income, and South Sea annuities more important still (bringing in variously £200–£400 per annum). However, the traffic in investments, especially consols, was in particular years especially brisk and the degree of short-term investment income varied accordingly. Between Morden's death and 1830 the ratio of investment to rental income was stable, but after this investment income was to increase in relative importance over rents. Nonetheless, the increase was slight, and in both the eighteenth and nineteenth centuries the overwhelming source of income was rent from land and property. Fee-farm rents were a minor element in rental income.

In the eighteenth century, as later, endowments supplemented College income: in 1822 for instance a brother of one of the trustees left £500 to the College.[3] The sale of College land was relatively uncommon: in 1807 lands previously rented by Greenwich Hospital were sold to the Hospital for £2,000,[4] but this and the 1827 sale to the New Cross Turnpike Trust (for £4,825) appear to have been the only major land sales made until the second half of the nineteenth century, when such sales become more common. With the exception of Greenwich Hospital, College tenants in the eighteenth century were private individuals (a number of them publicans). Income in the eighteenth century was further supplemented by profitable lease renewals and sales of such as timber and gravel from College property: Turnpike Trusts and the Board of Ordnance were the most important market for the latter.[5] The basis of the considerable fortune the estate was later to accrue lay in the careful management of land, and above all in the building lease. As early as 1723 leases were being vended with detailed clauses concerning the type and quality of building to be erected and the agricultural use to be made of land. The reversion of built property to the estate after the expiry of such leases was the chief means by which the fortunes of the College grew.

The trustees who managed College affairs were the mercantile and financial aristocracy of England. Nothing concerning the management of the estate is more interesting than the character of this involvement. For men skilled in buying and selling in a large range of markets the management of College affairs represented a kind of business holiday, a means by which skills acquired elsewhere could be refined at leisure. The geographical situation of the estate – on the perimeter of the growing city – also offered something of a microcosm of the regional land market, and thus a valuable means of acquiring expertise and connections in an area of commercial life to which the greater merchants were always drawn but in which first-hand knowledge was often limited. Philanthropic involvement considered as professional estate management was both a kind of hobby that perfected business practice and a valuable lesson in the rules of a new and lucrative area of the market.

The degree to which the expertise of the City was applied to College affairs with vigorous effect is apparent as early as 1712. It was then that the trustees set themselves the task of monitoring the College accounts in detail; then too that the decision was taken to restrict the period of leases so as to take full advantage of changes in the land market.[6] The character of estate management at Morden College differed considerably from that of so many eighteenth-century charities, at a time when some three-quarters of Britain's charitable trust income came from land. Many charities at the time – without the expertise Morden College could call on – failed to capitalise on increases in land values, and leased on long leases and low rents.[7] The building lease was the most characteristic expression of the acumen brought to College affairs: by the 1740s and 50s considerable sums were changing hands as the College leased house property that had now reverted to the estate.[8] The leases indicate a minute attention to the internal and external upkeep and development of the properties leased.[9]

In dealing with the College tenantry the trustees were no less eager to implement the principle of buying in the cheapest market and selling in the dearest. Of course the College was a charity and not a business house. Reduced rents might be allowed on land for a charity school,[10] and poor men and widows were sometimes allowed to accumulate arrears of rent.[11] This charity aspect was to be of more consequence in the next century, especially in relation to the local area. Though the charity was not a counting house what is most striking about the management of its estate is the way in which the values of the latter took precedence over the moral feeling inherent in the former. The degree to which men of business treated charity as a business is especially revealing, suggesting as it does that the canons of economic rationality, or at least expediency, pervaded and circumscribed the giving of the business classes. When it came to the essentials of profit and loss the paternalism seen in the sphere of social provision and social relations was often either absent or severely qualified.

A close scrutiny of College rent arrears was always made and warrants of distraint were frequently served upon the culprits.[12] These might include widows,[13] and those in arrears were imperiously called to give an account of themselves before meetings of the trustees.[14] The first survey of the estate was made in 1721,[15] and after this the attention of the trustees to College financial affairs was unrelenting. One measure of this attention was the visit of the trustees – men who were among the most notable of the City elite – to the houses of those tenants wishing to buy their properties.[16] Another reflection of this interest was the vigour with which the Crown's claim to rights in the property at Maidenstone Hill was contested.[17] In the 1750s these fourteen acres of land were the subject of a lawsuit so bitter and expensive that the trustees contemplated winding up the College.

The second great period of increase in the College fortunes – the 1820s and 30s – is reflected in the rental and dividend return for 1830–1; Rents, £3,913, Dividends, £991. Both sources of income grew steadily in importance thereafter (the 1860–1 rental was just over £5,000), but the really dramatic increase in rents came in the late 1870s: 1879–80 (c. £6,800), 1880–1 (c. £8,000), and 1890–1 (c. £11,100). Dividends also increased considerably in value between the 1860s and 90s, in 1890–1 standing at almost £1,900.[18] The increase of income in the

33

1820s and 30s coincided with the transfer of control from the Turkey Company to the East India Company in 1827. In the latter years of the Turkey Company period balances had accrued by dint of a considerable parsimony in College management. Expenses were kept down and the number of members kept at a minimum. In 1827 the East India Company took over a healthy annual surplus and in the years that followed the financial affairs of the College and estate were transformed, as the figures for annual income between 1830 and 1880 indicate. Between 1827 and 1837 almost £24,000 was invested from surplus income, and after 1850 the value of the estate was swollen by some considerable land sales, most notably those to the London, Chatham and Dover Railway in 1866 (£14,000), and the Naval Hospital, Greenwich in 1867 (£3,700). Despite the considerable costs of lawsuits in the East India Company period (between 1827 and 1845 these cost over £5,000), as well as the cost of College improvements, the foundations of the powerful financial position of the twentieth century were laid in the period of the East India Company.[19]

This transformation in College affairs owed everything to the transformation of the local area as industry and population moved outwards from the centre of London in the nineteenth century. The Charity Commissioners' report on Morden College in 1837 disclosed that the total number of properties held in Greenwich, Lewisham, Rochester and Chatham was 106. The Rochester estate, used chiefly for forestry revenue in the eighteenth century, was developed with building leases from 1817.[20] These returned an income of about £3,600, to which should be added fee-farm and pew rentals. The total income of the College was then just under £5,300.[21] By 1865, the date of the second parliamentary enquiry into the College,[22] working-class housing and industry had followed the early nineteenth-century growth of housing for the professional middle class in the area. Because of its closeness to London, and, as the report says, its strategic position for 'great public and industrial enterprises', the estate had become the site of extensive building. It was the leasing of land to builders of working-class housing but still more for industrial and commercial concerns in the area that led to the multiplication of College income. As we have seen, by the 1870s and 80s this building was impressively reflected in the estate rental. In 1865 the College estate included between 1,450 and 1,500 houses let on 229 mainly building leases. Most of this property was held in East Greenwich, Charlton, Lewisham and Rochester.

The Greenwich marshlands, chiefly leased to graziers and butchers in the early part of the century,[23] became the especially lucrative site of industry and public amenities for the growing population of London and the local area. Profits took the form of land sales as well as rents. These sales were usually a consequence of compulsory purchase orders, the policy of the trustees remaining one of conservation rather than active dealing in the land market. In 1884 the South Metropolitan Gas Company paid £12,300 into court for land in the Greenwich marshes, and in 1891 the L.C.C. purchased land for the Blackwall Tunnel. Land was also required by the London School Board and later the L.C.C. for the building of schools.[24] In 1905 electricity followed gas, and land was sold for the Greenwich Generating Station. Probably the most lucrative return of all was had from land bordering the river leased as wharves: in 1903 Associated Portland Cement was representative of the kind of tenant that now filled the College exchequer with some very substantial rents.[25] By 1907 a very great increase in trustee business concerning leases was reported,[26] an increase that resulted in a surveyors office being set up in South Street, Greenwich.[27] In 1920 the Chairman of the Trustees reported that the annual surplus was running at £10,000.[28]

The priorities of estate management in the eighteenth century were reflected in the nineteenth, and into the twentieth century as well. There was certainly a degree of somewhat paternalistic concern for the tenantry and the locale in the nineteenth century, but the same limitations in the economic sphere are again apparent. The trustees were quite happy to attend to the souls of their tenants, but their bodies had to be left to the vicissitudes of the market. In 1881, for instance, land was donated for a Mission House in Greenwich in the hope that the tenants in the area would benefit.[29] Nominal rents were charged to churches and schools in the 1880s, and money was donated to churches in areas where College property was held.[30] Not surprisingly, decayed gentlefolk outside the College had a special place in the trustees affections: in 1899 a Blackheath house was leased on a reduced rent to two ladies as a home for invalid 'gentlewomen'.[31] When, however, it came to the economic management of the estate the trustees had as keen an eye for profit as their eighteenth-century forebears.

In 1894 the Rochester town clerk reported that the Rochester properties were going to wrack and ruin.[32] House and other property had been let on repairing leases, and though notices to repair were served this was little consolation to tenants who had suffered decades of neglect from their own landlords and the College estate responsible for seeing that the terms of their own leases were kept to. In the other College properties conditions were little better. In 1908 the College Surveyor reported on the poor state of property in Greenwich and Blackheath,[33] the landlords again being allowed to go their own way by the College. Little seems to have been done in Rochester after the 1890s: in 1916 a trustee visited Rochester and reported that the estate there was not suitable for a charity to hold and should be sold.[34] Three years later, it being discovered that Corporation notices to repair could in fact be served on the College, a decision was made that it would be cheaper to sell.[35] In 1920 the properties were sold for about £21,000, and in 1926 most of the remaining Rochester land was disposed of.[36] In 1936 it was recent government legislation rather than its own concern that prompted the College to bring its housing up to standard by providing sculleries with sinks and a water supply.[37] As late as 1950 the worst parts of the estate were being let go, in this case Ladywell Park Estate to Lewisham Borough Council for £30,000.[38] A more solicitous attitude begins to be apparent in the

36

course of the Second World War when the tenants were allowed 'numerous indulgences' because of the time.[39] In the post-war years the quality of the large number of houses built and the attitude of the estate to the needs and wishes of the tenants has been in marked contrast with the long history of neglect.

The latter years of the nineteenth century were thus the boom ones from which the prosperity of the present century flowed. By 1896 something of the pattern of investment that was to characterise later years was apparent. In that year the College Surveyor recommended that freehold ground rents were a more stable form of investment than consols, and in the years that followed properties began to be acquired in the City.[40] In 1898 £22,087 was paid for a Bishopsgate property block.[41] Even so, in 1904 there was still £45,000 lodged with the courts on the College's behalf.[42] The dramatic increase of College fortunes in the nineteenth century was reflected in the scale of expenditure on the running of the College, and it is to the management of the College as opposed to the estate that we shall now turn.

In 1830–1 expenditure on pensions to members was £1,391, and on servants and nurses £413. Apothecaries' fees came to £68.[43] By 1860–1 expenditure on pensions had risen to £2,884 and that on servants and nurses to £858. The most marked increase in College expenditure however followed upon the great increase in rental income that we have noted in the 1870s. The creation of surplus income at this time resulted in the institution of out-pensions (in 1871) to those living outside the College but coming within the terms of eligibility of the members. By 1890–1 out-pensions accounted for £4,113 of expenditure, in fact more than members' pensions at £4,033. In the same year expenditure on servants, nurses and medical attendance was £1,178. The increased value of the estate was thus represented in the increasing size and complexity of the College itself: aside from the principal items of expenditure mentioned, costs of running and upkeep increased greatly between 1830 and 1900 as the number of members and pensioners grew and provision for the individual member was improved. By 1900 the College account stood at £15,977 for the year.[44]

This level of expenditure was eclipsed in the twentieth century as the estate prospered further and costs soared. By 1933 the total College account stood at £34,513, a figure which included £6,532 spent on members' pensions and £19,377 on out-pensions. Though the amount spent on pensions lessened greatly after the Second World War the costs of upkeep increased dramatically: £30,173 in 1960–1, £55,711 in 1970–1, and £157,453 in 1977–8 (College account balances). The practice of encouraging members' contributions developed in the 1960s, and in 1977–8 these stood at £22,557 of the total College account balance.

The major change in management policy after 1945 was the provision of rent-free accommodation in lieu of pension assistance. This was the result of the pre-war situation, when the advent of the National Assistance Board involved a clash

Public notice – '. . . for the purpose of electing two Merchants into the College . . .' *circa* 1820

of interest with the Scheme of organisation then in operation (it forbade College funds being used in relief of public funds). In 1960–1 the College Surveyor reported that £132,000 had been spent since 1959 on 43 flats for elderly married couples, 7 flatlets for elderly single women ('ladies as they are termed), and a Recreation Room and College Hospital extension.[45] It was further reported in 1975–6 that the trustees had provided homes in newly constructed buildings or specially purchased houses for 200 elderly people since 1949 at a cost of £1,033,250.[46] In 1977–8 only £13,532 was spent on out-pensions and a negligible amount on in-pensions. In 1977–8 expenditure on the running of the Morden College homes outside the College itself (the figures given above are for the College alone) amounted to £110,615 of a total joint expenditure balance for College and homes of £258,807, including out-pensions (the corresponding joint balance in 1970–1 was £88,569).[47]

The expansion of the College was made possible by the prosperity of the estate, a prosperity already being fostered by investment in City property at the end of the nineteenth century. This continued in the 1920s as well.[48] These strategies bore fruit in the very considerable increase in rental income in the immediate post-First War Years (from £24,500 in 1919 to £32,666 in 1920).[49] By 1949 the *gross* rental was £62,683 in the year, and by 1960–1 £118,920. The latter figure, together with dividends (at £12,617) and rent from subsidized property gave a total estate income of £143,735. The increase in rental in subsequent years was dramatic: the *nett* rental stood at £219,228 in 1970–1, and £484,163 in 1977–8.[50] As far back as 1949 the market value of investments stood at £545,000, though rental income now as always was far

38

greater than investment income. Most of these investments were in Savings Bonds, but also in War and British Transport stocks, and in Exchequer Bonds. This level of investment has been maintained into the present.

Between 1950–1 and 1977–8[51] the number of properties owned has increased from 1,195 to 1,340 (the latter figure does not include 238 garages). In terms of number City and West End properties have never been considerable in the period (15 in 1950–1, only 5 in 1975–6), but they have consistently brought a high return. In terms of return the riverside-industrial property has always mattered more – 36 properties in 1975–6 bringing in £70,000 as opposed to the City-West End return of £31,200. Weekly house lettings have been the most numerous, though they have decreased in number from 748 in 1950–1 to 568 in 1975–6. (Between 1936–8 an average of 907 of such weekly lettings were held.) In 1977–8 the 595 (now monthly) lets returned £66,733. Extensive redevelopment of house property began in 1953, many of the Greenwich properties in particular then being between 60 and 140 years old. By 1975–6 267 dwellings and 209 garages had been built at a cost of £1,135,750. These were of high quality and reasonable rent, the estate departing at last from a long history of unconcern in the management of its private, residential holdings. This building, as well as the new College building – as the Charity Commission's scheme of management laid down – was in large part financed out of surplus income and War Damage Value payments (amounting to some £100,000).[52] Between 1953 and 1976 316 houses had been demolished, and the improvement of old house property was speeded up after 1962.

One of the major post-war developments was the estate's activity in building subsidised dwellings (in 1957 the trustees were recognised as a housing association): between 1957 and 1975–6 '215 properties (flats and houses) and 116 garages had been completed at a cost of £821,233. In 1977–8 the slightly increased number of properties returned over £117,000 in rent, the largest single source of rental income. By then the estate's interests were diversified beyond housing and City-West End/Commercial-Industrial holdings. In 1950 the decision had been taken to buy shop property in small country towns in the South-East and in 'good class' suburban London situations. Such properties, including flats were sometimes used as business and professional premises as well, and continue to be a major source of income in the present.

References for Chapter Three

1. Morden College Account Book, 1708–68 (Bk. 89). On the Wricklemarsh estate see H. Lansdell, *Princess Aelfrida's charity* (1911, 1914), chap. XXVII; on the rental in Morden's time, chap. one, above.

2. Figures for College and Estate income from Accounts of Receipts and Disbursements/Cash Books: 1708–29 (Bk. 139), 1729–52 (Bk. 140), 1752–1806 (Bk. 141),

1806–1847 (Bk. 144). The annual income figures given here include balances brought forward. These balances are always less than *c.* 15 per cent of the annual income figure. See also Rent Ledger, 1716–18 (Bk. 137), Rent Book 1719–72 (Bk. 138), and Accnt. Book, 1708–68 (89). On College financial affairs see also Lansdell, *op. cit.*, chaps. XXX, XXXIII.

3. Morden College Minute Books, 24 October 1822.

4. Minutes: 2 February 1807.

5. Minutes: 16 August 1723.

6. Minutes: 15, 23 January 1712: leases were however later granted for periods longer than the twenty-one years mentioned at the latter meeting.

7. D. Owen, *English Philanthropy 1660–1960* (1965), pp. 72–3.

8. Minutes: 13 April 1742, 28 April 1752.

9. *Ibid.*, 6 July 1743, 8 June 1757.

10. *Ibid.*, 6 June 1807.

11. *Ibid.*, 16 December 1740, 29 April 1741.

12. E.g., 20 March 1753.

13. E.g., 24 April 1742.

14. E.g., 25 April 1759.

15. *Ibid.*, 7 February 1721.

16. *Ibid.*, 9 May 1723.

17. *Ibid.*, 31 October 1752, 2 January 1753, 6 October 1756; H. Lansdell, *op. cit.*, chap. XXX.

18. The most useful single source on College and estate finances in the nineteenth century is the MSS. Rent Roll, 1830–1 to 1899–1900 in M.C. Muniment Room. Detailed yearly accounts are available from 1873 in 'Expenses – Monthly Summary Books'. The annual accounts are interleaved in these.

19. On the nineteenth century financial affairs of Morden College see H. Lansdell, *op. cit.*, chaps. LVIII, LXIX, LXXI. For further information on income and expenditure in the nineteenth century, H. W. Smith (Treasurer of Morden College), 'The General Register of Morden College', MSS. Volume in Muniment Room.

20. Minutes: 3 December 1817.

21. Thirty-second Report of the Charity Commissioners, Pt. II, *Parliamentary Papers* 1837–8, XXVI (140), Report by Rt. Hon. Daniel Finch, pp. 842–862; see also Lansdell, *op. cit.*, chap. XLIII.

22. 'Correspondence between etc., etc. . . . conducted', *Parliamentary Papers* 1865, XLI (382), Report by Hare, pp. 170–6, on Morden College.

23. Minutes: 25 November 1814.

24. *Ibid.*, 14 February 1884 (see also 13 January 1881); Minutes: 1890–91, 1905.

25. *Ibid.*, 2 April 1903.

26. *Ibid.*, 3 October 1907.

27. 7 May 1914.

28. *Ibid.*, 2 December 1920.

29. 10 March 1881.

30. 7 May 1885, 20 May 1886.

31. 6 July 1899.

32. *Ibid.*, 25 October 1894.

33. 'Schedule referred to in Surveyor's Report, dated 3 March 1908', at end of Minute Book 8. 1905–13.

34. Minutes: 11 May 1916.

35. *Ibid.*, 8 May 1919.

36. *Ibid.*, 14 May 1920, 4 December 1926.

37. 5 March 1936.

38. Surveyor's Annual Report, 1950–1. In Clerk to the Trustees' Office.

39. Minutes: 16 November 1939.

40. *Ibid.*, 4 June 1896; 4 February 1897, 1 June 1899.

41. 5 May 1898.

42. 3 November 1904.

43. MSS. Rent Roll, 1830–1 to 1899–1900. Information on College management may be had from the Morden College Receipt Books, and the Disbursement Books. Both sets of books cover the century from 1708.

44. 'Expenses – Monthly Summary Book', 1900. Accounts interleaved.

45. College Surveyor's Annual Report, 1960–1.

46. *Ibid.*, 1975–6.

47. Morden College Annual Accounts, in Clerk to Trustees' Office, and deposited at Charity Commission.

48. Minutes: 1 June 1922.

49. 'Expenses – Monthly Summary Book', 1919, 1920. Figures include returnable income tax, at £4,685 in 1920.

50. Nett rental figures from Annual Surveyor's Reports.

51. This paragraph based on Surveyor's Reports, 1950–1 to 1977–8, Clerk to Trustees' Office.

52. Minutes: 15 January 1953.

ARMS OF THE TURKIE COMPANY

THe Company of *Merchants of Levant*, or (more commonly) termed *Turkie Merchants*, being firſt incorporated by Queene *Elizabeth*, were afterward confirmed and enlarged by our Soveraigne Lord King *Iames*.

Extract from *Survey of London*, 1633 edition, page 615, by John Stow.

CHAPTER FOUR

The World of Morden College I
– The Turkey Company Period,
1708–1826

By the terms of Sir John Morden's will the trustees and visitors of Morden College were to be chosen from the Turkey Company, and if this should cease to exist the East India Company. If the latter failed then the choice was to be from the Court of Aldermen of the City of London. Far-sighted in his claims upon posterity, in the unlikely event of the Court of Aldermen failing Morden decreed that seven '. . . discreet and grave . . . gentlemen of the County of Kent' should administer the College. A chaplain and treasurer were to manage daily affairs under the sole and absolute control of the trustees. It was the trustees' business to make new rules and amend old ones, and to examine into the behaviour, manner and religious observance of all officers, members and servants of the College.[1] This strict control was however exercised at a distance, the trustees visiting the College once a year, though meeting frequently at coffee houses, taverns and the headquarters of various livery companies to enact College and estate business.[2] It was this disposition of authority – absolute, but distanced, delegated and somewhat aloof – that was to be of such importance in defining the experience of College life for the members over the long span of the College's history.

The effect of this distanced control upon members whose experience was by definition one of failure was intensified by the characteristics of those in control over them, ones shaped primarily by success. The trustees were drawn from the highest level in City business life. The fifty or so trustees appointed during the Turkey Company period (the last one was appointed in 1817) were not only members of one of the great chartered companies but numbered often in their ranks baronets, directors of the Bank of England, Members of Parliament, as well as Lord Mayors.[3] Involvement with the College seems to have been of special importance to such men. Perhaps more than any contemporary institution Morden College was a reflection of City life, representing, as so many trustees liked to feel, the mercantile foundation of London's greatness. And Morden College was unique in this respect. In petitioning the Treasury Lords not to proceed with members' complaints in 1753 the trustees stated,

'... we flatter ourselves with the greater hopes ... as the wealth and strength of this kingdom depend upon commerce, and ours is the only charity for merchants who have been so unfortunate, as to have been ruined by the carrying of it on ...'[4] Situated close to London, and in a neighbourhood rich in naval and maritime associations, the College was especially close to the heart of the City patriciate.

This interest was reflected in the markedly familial character of trusteeships in the period. Just like the family business, trusteeships were handed down from father to son. In this period four Bosanquets, four Cookes, three Chiswells and three Lees were numbered among the trustees. If scrutiny of College affairs was distanced, then it was often accompanied by a high degree of inherited, personal knowledge. This example highlights the very important place of the family in charity over the centuries. When the administration and dispensation of charity is understood in terms of unofficial patronage links, then the family, as a means of ordering such networks, can be seen to have its special importance.[5] By the terms of John Morden's will his and his wife's kin were to be preferred for any office at Morden College. Examples of this kind of preferment – from the highest to the most menial office – abound in the history of Morden College. Thus the charitable foundation itself provided a niche for the poor relation, just as the trusteeship provided a niche (often inherited) in the higher reaches of London charity. The degree to which colleges and almshouses provided both outdoor and indoor relief for tribes of founders' and indeed governors' kin is unknown, though going on the history of Morden College it cannot have been inconsiderable. As a consequence of the family link, institutions like Morden College, already closed and introspective, were made even more intimate and all-pervading.

The first two treasurers of the College, Nathaniel and Joseph Brand, were relations of Lady Morden. The force of kin loyalty is reflected in Joseph being made treasurer, in 1728, after Nathaniel had been found out in defrauding the College. When Joseph Brand was elected another poor relation of the founders canvassed for the job, and was rewarded with six guineas for his pains. The next clan of treasurers was the Bennetts, John, Thomas and Alexander Bennett being grandsons of Lady Morden's youngest sister, who married as her second husband another custodian of charity to the once-respectable poor, Sir John Bennett, Judge in the Marshalsea Court and later Steward of the Marshalsea prison for debtors. Between them the Brands and their cousins the Bennetts held the post of treasurer at the College from 1708 to 1819.[6]

After Sir John Morden's death the semi-patriarchal unity of the College household broke apart, the College settling into a less patriarchal but equally hierarchic system of authority, one more in keeping with the operation of a charitable institution than Morden's version of household organisation had

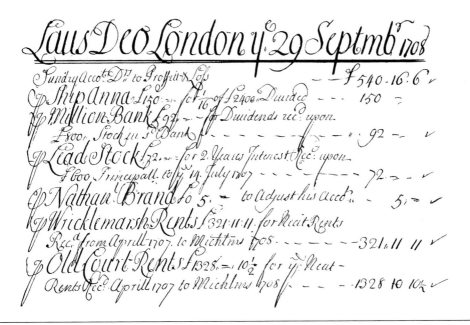

Entries made on September 29th, 1708, in one of the two First Account Books shortly after the death of Sir John Morden on September 6th, 1708. The second entry refers to the ship *Anna* in which Sir John had an interest

been. The merchants were marked off more completely in their domain as gentlemen, after 1727 the members and servants ceasing to eat together. The stipulation in the original rules that the chaplain and treasurer should take their diet with the members does not seem to have been observed in these years: only in 1819 do we find the treasurer deciding to dine again with the members, significantly enough, in the interests of the 'good government and advantage of the Institution'.[7] In the eighteenth century the treasurer and chaplain saw to most aspects of quotidian College affairs. Indeed, in the 1790s the trustees were leaving much of the discretion over admittance into the College in the hands of the treasurer, aside from his various responsibilities in running the College and estate (keeping the books, collecting rents, overseeing the provisioning of the members). The treasurer and chaplain were responsible to the trustees for the discipline and good order of the College, the chaplain in particular being responsible for determining disputes between members and relaying the dictates of the trustees to the pensioners.

This combination of secular and spiritual supervision made the chaplain perhaps the most influential figure in eighteenth century College life. His spiritual responsibilities were alone immense, by the terms of the founder's will the maximum number of services each year at which he could be called to officiate being more than one thousand.[8] By the terms of the founder's rules, and under threat of ten days loss of 'commons' or diet, the members had to attend morning and evening service in their gowns, and – prayer-book in hand – always to behave with great piety and dignity in chapel. Communion was to be taken four times a year, again under penalty of loss of commons. The 'expositions' and evening lectures also had to be attended. The rigour of this religious régime was by no means untypical of the time, being seen in similar institutions like Norfolk College, Bromley College and Charterhouse. It was only a little moderated by the revised rules of 1821.[9] For this expenditure of energy the chaplain was handsomely rewarded. His salary was supplemented by rents from the chaplain's field (money for which was donated by Lady Morden), pew rents, special gratuities from the trustees, and rights to the proceeds from the sale of estate produce.[10] In the eighteenth century the College chaplaincy was among the best paid in the country. As was so often the case, positions of authority carried a measure of patronage, and the chaplaincy was no exception. The son of Moses Browne, chaplain between 1763 and 1787 (and a friend of Dr Johnson), applied with success to have the College buy his goods.[11] He was by trade a woodturner. As with the position of treasurer, kinship with the founders was the surest way to preferment. Immediately after the century-long reign of the Brands and Bennetts, a succession of four chaplains who were all kin of the founder's wife began in 1819.

Throughout the eighteenth century the College chapel was the only Anglican place of worship in the immediate neighbourhood, and to it must have come a number of the local population, rich and poor. Though for a later period (the 1830s to the 1860s) the chapel baptismal register refers to servants, gardeners and labourers christening their children at the College.[12] Many of these would have been the servants and workmen of well-to-do local inhabitants, but others would have been College servants, in the eighteenth century as well as in the nineteenth. That the rites of passage were marked by the College itself serves to indicate that the authority of the chaplain and treasurer was exerted over servants as well as members, and that the servants were in many ways as integral a part of College life as the members. Indeed, despite the separation of aspects of the members' lives from those of the servants in the eighteenth century, the servants lived in the College, cheek by jowl with the members and those in authority over them. To appreciate the role of the servants in the makeup of the College the following representation of organisational structure will be useful.

Though the servants ate separately from the members (appointing their own caterers in much the same fashion), their lodging, diet and wages were provided by the College. Very much a part of the institution's life, they attended to all the daily needs of an aged, sometimes ill, and often demanding membership. Though gratuities to servants were not permitted, they seem frequently to have

The Organisation of Morden College in the Eighteenth and Nineteenth Centuries

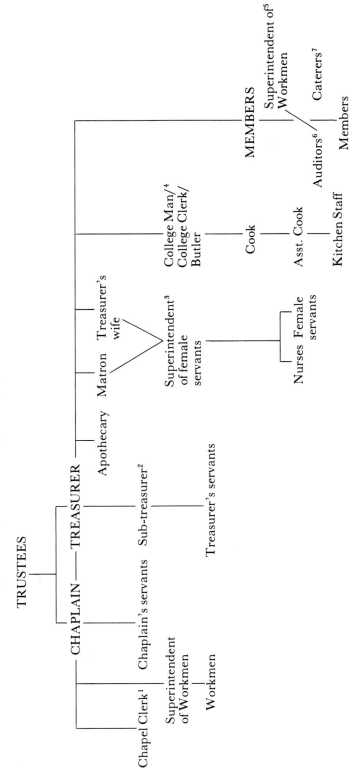

1. Chapel Handyman, College barber, in early eighteenth century also butler.
2. At various times in the nineteenth century called 'Visitor', and responsible for manual duties in College; Sub-treasurer at other times clerical assistant to treasurer.
3. In nineteenth century married to College Clerk/Butler, and called Matron. Separate Matron in eighteenth century.
4. College Man, a general labourer and College handyman, seems to have been upgraded to College Clerk and thence Butler in the nineteenth century.
5. Sometimes chosen from among members.
6. & 7. Elected by members and responsible for catering arrangements at the different tables.

47

The Rev Moses Browne,

Chaplain of Morden College,
1763–1787
The College possesses a copy of
the 1750 edition of Izaak
Walton's *The Compleat Angler*
which was edited by Moses
Browne who, to quote from
the preface, undertook the
work 'Accordingly, at the insti-
gation of a very ingenious and
learned friend . . .

(Mr Samuel Johnson)

been given. Hired directly by the chaplain and treasurer, the servants as much as the members were circumscribed by those in authority over them. Servants had to be back in College before nightfall. In the 1760s both the College Man and the Chapel Clerk were dismissed for drunkenness and absence without permission.[13] The elements of preferment and family connection were once again apparent. In 1756 a poor relation of Lady Morden was made Cook.[14] At other times daughter might follow mother as College Cook.[15] The letter of recommendation was all important: in 1758 a new Cook was taken on on the strength of the 'recommend' of one of the local gentry, Lady Page.[16].

The provision made for aged and ill servants reveals something of the character of the College régime. The paternalism in evidence here, though more notable than that in the sphere of estate management, was nonetheless qualified by economic considerations. Long and faithful service was needed to qualify for special treatment. In order to prevent 'indiscriminate' doles to poor, ill servants it was decided in 1764 that all future servants should produce a certificate of settlement from the parish responsible for them. At the same time the College came to an arrangement with Charlton parish to reimburse the Poor Law

48

authorities for all servants given a settlement in that parish.[17] But if the College's responsibility for its own was therefore a measured one, when special loyalty was in question it was often rewarded with doles and pensions.[18] Old servants were also occasionally permitted to continue in residence after the end of their working lives.[19] For all servants there were generous gratuities from the trustees on Visitation Day and at Christmas.

Although full information on the membership is only available from the early nineteenth century onwards,[20] it is clear, that in the eighteenth century and for most of the nineteenth century the stipulation that only merchants engaged in overseas trade should be admitted was strictly adhered to. The like of wine dealers, gold and silver lace dealers, and a butcher and farmer were all rejected as inadmissible in the early nineteenth century.[21] The taboo on mere retailers was absolute. The method of application was by petition read to the trustees at their coffee house meetings either by the applicant or, more often, by an advocate of his. The force of the letter of recommendation was overwhelming and therefore the influence of the referee all important. Letters of good conduct had to be forthcoming from 'respectable' friends, City figures and merchants. The trustees depended for their information on the known and tightly-organised world of the City. The more influential was the source of information the more likely was it to be listened to. When a petitioner had the support of one of the trustees themselves he could be assured of a specially attentive hearing.[22] For the most part, however, the fate of the candidates was decided in terms of the network of high-society contacts and friendships that spanned the City and the trustees. Many of the applicants were livery company members, and the companies themselves, especially by means of contact between their superior liverymen, were an important link in this network.

The men who applied to Morden College were nearly always destitute. Their fall from grace had often happened long before they applied for admission, and in the interim many had engaged in the most menial tasks. The provision made for College members was a badge of their status as once men of worth and now gentlemen of a sort again. It was generous, and in striking contrast with the kind of life the poor were expected to lead in charitable institutions. As we have seen, members in Morden's day were allowed accommodation, food, the care of servants and nurses, allowances for coal, candles and gowns, as well as a money allowance.[23] Although Morden was forced to reduce the allowance it was increased to generous levels in the course of the century.[24] Members were also allowed periodic doles, such as those on Visitation Day. As usual, poor relations of the Mordens were not forgotten: they might be given money doles or gifts of clothing.[25] A sharp eye was nonetheless kept on expenses. By the Rules and Orders of 1807 the treasurer was enjoined to proceed in works and repairs with 'caution and prudence as Charity money ought to be managed'. It was one of the Sub-treasurer's responsibilities to see that the fire in the Hall was not kept too high in the evenings.

In the course of the nineteenth century the allowance – from which money for dinner had to be paid – was raised until it reached £100 per annum in 1881. Money for washing and candles was also provided then, as well as coal and wood for fires, bread and ale, and furniture up to £25 in value. Each member had a sitting room, a sleeping room and a cellar. By then the College was provided with a library, a recreation room, and a new dining hall (begun in 1844).[26] In line with the improved provision for members in the nineteenth century went an improvement in the status of members which material advances in turn enhanced: in 1819 it was decided that members should henceforth be called 'gentlemen pensioners'.[27] The chronically ill were not accepted as members, indeed under the founder's rules those with infectious diseases were to be expelled. Though an apothecary was appointed in the 1720s, and nursing was provided for sick members, the authorities again reflected the limitations of their sense of responsibility by attempting to get the relatives of the chronically ill to look after them (with the aid of a small annual donation).[28] The ban on relatives residing in College was relaxed only when members were chronically ill or unable to help themselves. It was not until well into the nineteenth century that medical care was provided in anything like an adequate manner.

The institutional order in which the members lived can best be appreciated by a consideration of the College Rules. Only poor merchants who were 'honest, sober and discreet members of the Church of England' were admissible. They had to be unmarried or widowed, and not less than fifty years of age (under the founder's original rules). Those admitted had to be genuine casualties of business life and not men brought to their ruin by their own personal failings; as the rules put it, 'merchants fallen to decay by accidents of the sea or otherwise in their way of merchandizing'. Something of the rigour with which the members were exhorted to respectability and piety has been seen in the religious régime of the College. Those not measuring up to the criteria for admission if inadvertently admitted were to be expelled immediately, as were 'any common swearers, drunkards, quarrelsome, debauched and disorderly persons . . .'.[29] Members were to be in constant residence, and 'not to be wandering about tipling in public and disorderly houses, but to employ themselves in acts of piety and devotion . . .'. The maximum leave of absence was twenty-four hours. The gates were locked at nine in the summer and eight in the winter. Most pertinent of all, members were not to 'intermeddle with the business of the College', but to 'demean themselves civilly, without ill language, strife or disturbance'. The whole disciplinary structure was maintained by a system of fines (loss of privileges and 'commons' or diet), by suspension, and by the ultimate sanction of expulsion.[30]

50

Example of a typical application for entry into Morden College. Applicants were evidently given guidance as to choice of wording as almost all commence with the same opening phrase

This system had changed little by 1821, the date of the first major revision of College rules.[31] Far from moderating the severity of discipline, members were now to be expelled for bringing women into the College or marrying. The condemnation of drunkenness was made with all the ardour of the original rules. By the new rule eight, '. . . if any member of the College sits up drinking at unseasonable hours in the night, or gets drunk in and out of the College, or be led home, or found, or known to be in that beastly condition which is not only a prejudice to his own health, but a public scandal to the government of the College . . .' then such a man was to be reported to the trustees at once for their most severe correction. The way in which the attack upon drunkenness and the exhortation to submissiveness and respectability were pressed home throughout the eighteen and nineteenth centuries suggests that if the discipline imposed was harsh and severe, then it was resented and circumvented by the members, many of whom were neither sober nor discreet. The reactions of the gentlemen merchants to this discipline and dependence presents one of the most interesting faces of College history.

Compared with the acute interest in the moral well-being of servants and members shown in the nineteenth century, the early eighteenth century was a period of relative slackness. Under the treasurership of the Brands to 1757 the College went through a period of financial restriction too, in which economies were made in the use of servants and the provision of medical care.[32] Defoe

51

himself commented on the run-down condition of the College in its early years. Nonetheless, the keen business sense of the trustees, who were among the elite of City business life, quickly led to the upturn in College fortunes we have charted in the previous chapter. The degree of slackness in College affairs – reflected in laxity over the residence rule, and married men having College benefits[33] – also gave way in the second quarter of the century to the more forceful moral oversight that was to characterise most of the College's history. This low point in the early history of the College was symbolised by the discovery of the treasurer Nathaniel Brand's corruption: he was discovered in 1729 profiting from the Land Tax returns to the tenantry.[34] The deficiencies in organisation and discipline in the early years were reflected in the generality of charities throughout most of the century, a century characterised by trustee mismanagement, even peculation,[35] and the near-total unconcern of the State in the affairs of charitable foundations.[36]

Morden College, however, seems to have been less culpable than most. The intensification of discipline took the form of the carrot and the stick. Gratuities were paid to members as an encouragement to live 'well and orderly'. These were lost for quarrelling, and for 'impudent and repeated misbehaviour'.[37] Though there was only one Visitation Day a year it was a pretty thorough event. The trustees personally inspected every apartment and the conduct of every member. Thus the gratuities of Visitation Day were complemented by the moral scrutiny of that day, and erring members might also be called to give an account of themselves at the trustees' coffee house meetings.[38] A new means of maintaining order makes its appearance in the 1770s. In 1778 the office of 'Visitor' was filled from among the membership. In the following year another pensioner was made overseer of the college workmen.[39] These offices, and the subsequent one of deputy-visitor, formed something like a prefectorial system in the College. These officers reported on the members' misconduct to the trustees, and were paid small amounts for their trouble (the 'Visitor' got 40 shillings a year). They certainly had some standing in College life: in 1789 a member was expelled for his 'impudence' to a visitor.[40] Something of the trustees' attitudes to the members about this time is apparent from their idea of their political status: in 1802 the trustees felt called upon to forbid members to vote at parliamentary elections. In an assertion of their individual worth as citizens, members had exercised their right to vote despite the trustees considering them ineligible by virtue of their dependent status.[41]

The response of the members to all this was many-sided. Reactions to the religious order of the College show the complexity of their attitudes. The high-handedness of 'absentee' trustees, and the moral discipline exerted upon gentlemen fallen from grace to dependence could excite a considerable degree of resistance to authority. On the other hand, the need for order and status among

52

The Rev. George Pattrick
Chaplain of Morden College
1787–1790

His excessive zeal and inclina-
tion towards Methodism led to
disputes with the College
members and to his ultimate
dismissal. Later he became a
lecturer at St Bride's, Fleet
Street and also shared a
lectureship at St Margaret's,
Lothbury. As a preacher he was
popular and drew large congregations. He had a strong voice
and clear enunciation

men who had tasted disaster and humiliation could bolster the solidarity of the institution. Religion, or rather the defence of the Anglican Establishment, seems to have worked to these ends. The desire for order found expression in a privileged and patriotic religion which sanctified the secular standing and worth of merchants, individually as well as collectively. This is especially apparent in the chaplaincy of the Rev. George Pattrick from 1787.[42] Pattrick's Methodism was at odds with the orthodoxy of the members and trustees alike. For the members, orthodoxy was a major criterion of their admission to the College. On the evidence of Morden College at least, the heterodoxy of the London merchant community in the seventeenth century had given way to a much clearer orthodoxy in the eighteenth.

An earlier chaplain, Moses Browne, had created some dismay by his Evangelical zeal, but in 1790 Pattrick drew the full wrath of the College upon himself, nineteen out of twenty-seven members signing a petition against his 'Methodism'.[43] The petition was eagerly accepted by the trustees and Pattrick was hounded from the chaplaincy. He went on to be a very successful City preacher, and a member of the Eclectic Society and the Church Missionary

Society that was formed out of it. The attack on Pattrick had, however, to do with other aspects of his religion than its nonconformity. Because there was no other church in the area Pattrick's services and sermons drew people from the neighbourhood. Pattrick also held meetings at his home, three times a week, at which extemporary prayers were said 'by many of the lower classes of people to the number of forty or fifty at a time . . .'[44] To men very conscious of the degree of standing restored to them by College membership this aspect of Pattrick's mission was as offensive as his attack upon formal orthodoxy. In the face of this offence to their dignity the members closed rank with those in authority over them.

This definition of their own worth in terms of those below them in the social hierarchy was clearly at all times of the greatest importance in securing order and a more positive credence in the moral authority of the institution as a community of gentlemen merchants. This consciousness of superiority over the poor tended to complement the effect of dependence that was forced home by the authoritarian rigour of the College régime. It also accorded with the need for order and standing among men aware of their loss and of the perilous restoration of security. Thus there were clearly many years in which the tenor of College life was calm and uninterrupted, and many members for whom the hierarchic and authoritarian order of the College was the source of a stability which belief in this order's rightness and inevitability brought. But there were other years and other men, and what is so striking, given the kind of institution the College was, one catering for the dependent who had embraced a fair measure of good order, respectable obedience, and regularity of habit in their working lives, is the very powerful current of disorder, disobedience and resistance that runs through its history. Though worldly success had gone, there remained still the precious notion of the merchant as gentleman. That notion was always the most sensitive to trustee condescension and to severe discipline. It was when it was not sufficiently acknowledged by authority that the members were stung into opposition.

This opposition in the eighteenth century took several forms, most of them fairly unorganised and spontaneous. The exception was the lawsuit against the trustees. In 1743 some 'turbulent spirits' among the members decided to act against the trustees for not providing a pension in line with their station in life and with the financial resources of the College.[45] The trustees summarily refused to hear their petition and the case went to court. It was dismissed, though this is hardly surprising as the trustees refused to let the members see the College books and so prepare a proper case. The aftermath of the case shows the power at the trustees disposal and their willingness to use it: the three chiefly involved in the move were subsequently harried by the trustees, and two of them were expelled despite begging for mercy. The fate faced by those expelled was invariably renewed destitution. The trustees sometimes provided support for a man expelled, as with a man found stealing in 1796.[46] The pension provided was, however, meagre, and even this might be refused if the member involved was in the eyes of the trustees an unseemly and difficult character.[47]

Not a few of the members in the eighteenth century were in fact difficult characters. The severity with which the membership were exhorted to good order only made them more determined to bring bad order into their lives and that of the College. This disorder was a kind of inchoate, semi-organised rebellion against authority. It was compounded by the anarchy of the aged, a desire among men near the end of their lives to do things in their way rather than in the way so long expected of them. This element of feeling may have been strong among men who had lived their lives according to the strict, or at least outwardly strict, rules of business life. Though the members who were admitted only after the most careful scrutiny had decided it was fortune and not their own vice that had led to their fall, it is probable that a number of the wayward would have found their way in. And these men would have carried their waywardness into College life.

The members' opposition was the product of weakness rather than strength, and one of the few half-organised foci available to it, as in many such institutions, was the dinner table. The dinner table was the source of a life within the life of the institution. The Caterers and Auditors who organised the provision of dinner at the College were chosen by the members, though paid by the treasurer. These enjoyed a considerable freedom in going to market, buying the food, overseeing its preparation, and seeing that the 'overplus' in money was divided up equitably among the members. All members could expect to fill these offices. Thus for the membership this system introduced an important element of self-determination concerning meal-times, perhaps the most significant social occasions in all such small-scale institutions. The Morden College table was divided into three separate tables, each of which had a life of its own. This life can be understood in much the same way as the house in a public school – as a mechanism ensuring the *esprit de corps* of the whole institution – but more often it seems to have been the source of counter-attacks upon order. This is apparent in the 'embroils' at table that punctuated College history.[48]

Most of the discontent took forms that had no organisational centre at all and were a spontaneous expression of opposition. This is apparent in a degree of sexual licence that even by the latitudinarian standards of the time was notable. In 1751 the trustees laid down 'that upon information, that some of the Pensioners by bringing women into their apartments in the Colledge, have catched the Itch, that if any hereafter shall do ye same, that they be expelled.'[49] This laxity, however, seems to have been less marked than non-residence as a form of indiscipline. In 1776 there was a purge of the non-resident, after it was discovered that many were living outside the College. One man even let his apartment to his niece, and another (dubiously or not) spent his time in London collecting charity subscriptions. At least one member was expelled.[50] The prohibition on the social intercourse of the sexes was often made: in 1819 a member's wife was thrown out for being resident and for mixing with the members.[51] Keeping the servants and members in their separate stations, and in their separate rooms, seems to have been no less of a problem. Insulting behaviour is often reported in the minutes. No doubt some of this was the work of old men who were difficult in the extreme. What we are to make of a case of improper behaviour and language to poor children in 1794 is unclear,[52] and the abuse given to nurses must often have been the product of the cantankerousness of old age.[53] Some members were notorious, one Fox Smith in 1801 being especially unruly, insulting the nurses, and keeping a boy in his apartment.'[54] Members might also be in a 'dirty and nasty' condition.[55] The penalties for these offences were harsh, though harsher still for those insulting figures of authority.

By far the most important expression of discontent and refractory behaviour was the members' insistence not only on not being 'responsible', but on being 'unrespectable' in a drunken manner. Drunkenness is perhaps the most persistent theme in the misconduct of College members, from the earliest days right into the twentieth century. In the early part of the eighteenth century this was not surprising, the beer allowance being two quarts a day. In 1721 a certain widow Begg was to be shown the College gates if she sold any more beer or brandy on the premises,[56] and about the same time members were fined for buying more than a quart of gin at a time.[57] Expulsion was the punishment for the third offence, a sanction also exercised for disorderly and foul-mouthed

56

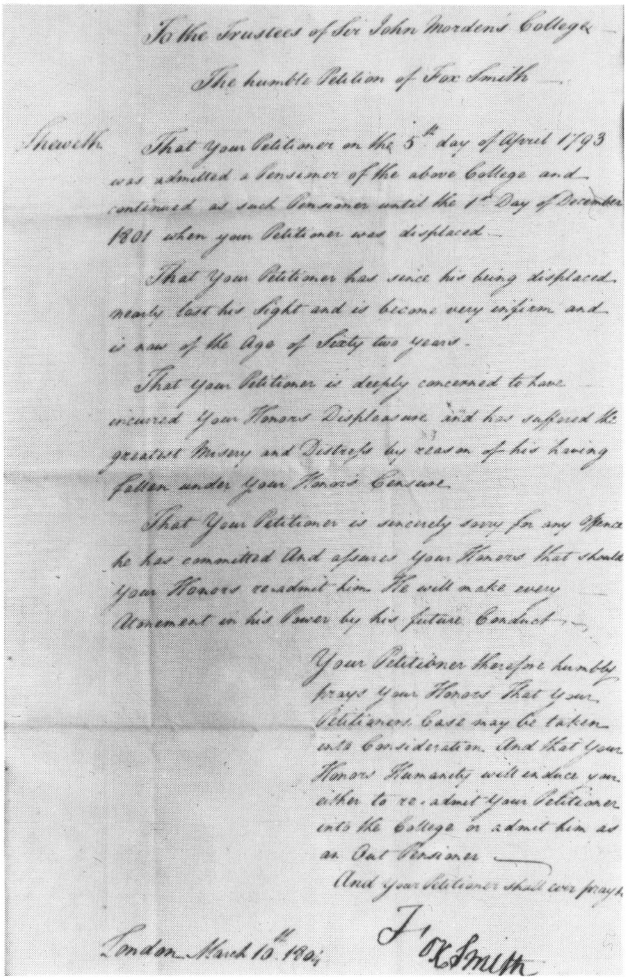

Petition of a former member to re-enter the College. Fox Smith had been expelled for unruly and insulting behaviour in 1801

[Handwritten petition reproduced at right:]

To the Trustees of Sir John Morden's College

The humble Petition of Fox Smith

Sheweth That your Petitioner on the 5th day of April 1793 was admitted a Pensioner of the above College and continued as such Pensioner until the 1st Day of December 1801 when your Petitioner was displaced

That Your Petitioner has since his being displaced nearly lost his sight and is become very infirm and is now of the age of sixty two years.

That your Petitioner is deeply concerned to have incurred Your Honors Displeasure and has suffered the greatest Misery and Distress by reason of his having fallen under Your Honors Censure.

That Your Petitioner is sincerely sorry for any Offence he has committed And assures Your Honors that should your Honors readmit him He will make every Atonement in his Power by his future Conduct

Your Petitioner therefore humbly prays Your Honors that your Petitioners Case may be taken into Consideration And that Your Honors Humanity will induce you either to re-admit Your Petitioner into the College or admit him as an Out Pensioner

And your Petitioner shall ever pray

London March 10th 1804

Fox Smith

behaviour.[58] Members' behaviour was so great a problem that in 1740 a system of fines was brought in for drunkenness. The 1740 Rules and Orders also inveighed against those 'living on the Heath in that beastly condition'.[59] The fines imposed made little difference, and an examination of the College Minutes in the 1740s and 50s shows a constant stream of reprimands and expulsions for drunken and violent behaviour.[60] As we have seen, College servants were not immune from the prevailing order of things.

One of the first actions taken by the treasurer H. W. Smith on taking up his position in 1819 was to forbid drink to the College workmen.[61] This was to be the augury of a determined, and largely unsuccessful, attack on the central role that drink had in College life. Much more than this, however, Smith's treasurership was to see the stirrings of the early-Victorian conscience as it applied itself to Morden College no less than to society at large. The developing mania for bestowing moral improvements was to make itself felt with particular force from the beginnings of the period of the East India Company's trusteeship, and it is these years that we shall now consider.

References for Chapter Four

1. Rules and Orders, Morden College, *c*. 1700, Morden College Muniment Room.

2. In the early eighteenth century, before trustee meetings were regularised, the incidence of meetings depended on the amount of College, though usually estate business that had to be transacted. In the fifteen years to 1722 there were 46 meetings, in the fifteen years 1723–1737, 113 meetings.
Cf. Minute Books for details, Muniment Room, M.C.

3. For biographical information and sources on the trustees, see H. Lansdell, *Princess Aelfrida's Charity* (2 vols. 1911, 1914, 7 parts), chap. XXVII, also XLV, XLVI. For the list of trustees in the period see Appendices below.

4. Minutes: 2 January 1753; see also 11 May 1770.

5. See above, chap. 2.

6. On the two families, H. Lansdell, *op. cit.*, chaps. XXVIII, XXXIII.

7. Minutes: 9 December 1819.

8. H. Lansdell, *op. cit.*, chap. XL, p. 66.

9. 'Abstract of Rules and Orders to be observed by the Members, Caterers and Auditors of Morden College' (1821), Muniment Room. See also Lansdell, chaps. XVII, XXXVII.

10. On the eighteenth and early nineteenth century chaplains, Lansdell, chaps. XXV, XXXI, XXXIV (esp. p. 42), and chap. XL.

11. Minutes: 16 February 1764.

12. Register of Baptisms at Morden College, 1793 onwards in 'Second Register, Obituary Book', M.C. Muniment Room.

13. Minutes: 12 July 1761; also 23 June 1762, and June 1763.

14. Minutes: 28 April 1756.

15. Minutes: 2 December 1755.

16. *Ibid.*, 1 March 1758.

17. 23 June 1764.

18. E.g., 1 March 1758; 2 August 1789; 17 July 1809.

19. 9 August 1820.

20. 'First Register of Admissions, *c.* 1702–1791', M.C. Muniment Room: no entries to 1774, thereafter only bare details of names, dates of birth, death, etc. Not until the nineteenth century 'Register of Applications' is systematic analysis possible.

21. H. Lansdell, *op. cit.*, chap. XXIX, p. 64.

22. Minutes: 15 March 1758.

23. See above, p.

24. H. Lansdell, *op. cit.*, chap. XXXIV; Minutes: 26 February 1824.

25. Minutes: 15 December 1736, 26 April 1738.

26. Cf. 1867 and 1881 Rules and Orders, Muniment Room; Minutes: 10 November 1825 (Kelsall Library bequest), 24 June 1875 (recreation room), 31 December 1844 (grounds to be laid out).

27. Minutes: 17 July 1819.

28. Minutes: 19 March 1772, 25 February 1774; see also, 13 December 1738.

29. Founder's Rules and Orders.

30. Founder's Rules and Orders, *c.* 1700, Muniment Room.

31. 1821 Rules and Orders, Muniment Room.

32. H. Lansdell, *op. cit.*, chap. XXVIII.

33. *Ibid.*, chaps. XXIX, XXXIII, also Minutes: 15 March 1758.

34. Minutes: 9 May 1729.

35. B. Kirkman Gray, *A History of English Philanthropy* (1905), pp. 225–7.

36. D. Owen, *English Philanthropy 1660–1960* (1965), Pt. I, chap. 3.

37. Minutes: 5 May 1736.

38. Minutes: 28 November 1739, also Lansdell, chap. **XXXIV**.

39. Minutes: 15 July 1778; 30 September 1779.

40. *Ibid.*, 16 February 1789; see also Minutes for 1794.

41. Lansdell, chap. **XXXIV**.

42. For biography of Pattrick, *ibid.*, chap. **XXXII**.

43. For the full story see Minutes for 1790, esp. March–June.

44. Minutes: 24 February 1790.

45. For a full account Minutes: 25 May 1744, Lansdell, ch. **XXIX**.

46. Minutes: 15 April 1796.

47. See the case of Fox Smith, 10 July 1801.

48. E.g., 19 May 1736.

49. Minutes: 6 August 1751.

50. Minutes: 10 July 1776, 17 October 1776.

51. *Ibid.*, 17 July 1819.

52. 30 May 1794.

53. Lansdell, chap. **XXXIV**.

54. Minutes: 10 July, 27 November 1801.

55. Minutes: 25 April 1759.

56. Minutes: 7 September 1721.

57. Lansdell, chap. **XXIX**.

58. *Ibid.*, also chap. **XXXIV**; see esp. Minutes: 11 January 1733, 25 April 1733.

59. Minutes: 2 May 1740; 1740 Rules and Orders, Muniment Room.

60. Minutes: 23 June 1742; 30 November 1743; 10 April 1744; 19 November 1751.

61. *Ibid.*, 3 May 1820.

ARMS OF THE EAST INDIA COMPANY

THe Company of Merchants, called *Merchants of Eaſt-India*, were incorporated by Queene *Elizabeth*, *Anno Dom.* 1600.

Extract from *Survey of London*, 1633 edition, page 617, by John Stow

CHAPTER FIVE

The World of Morden College II
– The East India Company Period,
1827–1884

The Turkey Company trustees were drawn from the upper reaches of the City in which high finance and mercantile capital had long been wedded. The growing intimacy of this union in the nineteenth century is reflected in the character of the trustees in the East India Company period. Numbering the Barings, Lubbocks and Thorntons in their ranks, the new trustees were even more evidently the aristocracy of money than the old.[1] The convergence of economic interests, and the emergence of this aristocracy, owed everything to the development of London as the money market of the world.[2] The family character of College trusteeships was even more in evidence than in the eighteenth century, reflecting the resilience of the family connection in embracing and ordering a capitalism that was substantially more complex and interdependent in organisation than its eighteenth-century predecessor. It is not until the twentieth century, and its more anonymous and institutionalised modes of administration, that the family ceded precedence as a principle of political and social as well as economic organisation. The character of the trustees in this period indicates the way in which College government was very much a microcosm of Victorian City big business.

The first East India Company trustee was William Astell, a Thornton who had changed his name in 1807. Chairman of the Russia and East India Companies, his chairmanship of the Great Northern Railway illustrates not only the movement of mercantile capital into the institutional world of the investment and financial markets, but also the increasingly unified economic life of the nation itself, of which the old merchant aristocracy was now very much a part. The son of a director of the Bank of England, he began his parliamentary career as M.P. for Bridgnorth in 1800, represented it during six successive parliaments, and served for the remainder of his life as Conservative member for Bedfordshire, where he was Deputy Lieutenant for the county. Colonel of the Royal East India Volunteers, he ended his twenty-two year trusteeship at the College in 1847. He was succeeded by another Thornton, John, a partner in the banking house of Williams, Deacon and Co. On the death of his elder brother he succeeded to the title of ninth Earl of Leven and eighth Earl of Melville, a prime example of the long-established accessibility of the City to aristocratic society. Thorntons were represented on the Board of Trustees at Morden College for the whole of this period, John Thornton being followed by his son in 1875. Their continuous interest was paralleled by the Lubbocks, opulent City merchants and bankers. John Lubbock, who established the family banking house, was made a baronet in 1806. Son succeeded father as Turkey Company trustee in 1811, and the third baronet, educated at Eton and Trinity College, Cambridge, became a trustee in 1840. Sir John William Lubbock was the first Vice-Chancellor of London University. This philosophical and scientific *amateur* was succeeded as a trustee by his son John in 1865, family service to the College extending for almost a hundred years.

The continuity existing between the two periods of trusteeship was represented by the Bosanquet family as well, four of whom were trustees in the earlier, Turkey Company period. Of the two who spanned both periods, Charles was Governor of the South Sea Company as well. He split his time between town and country, as did so many of his equals, residing at Hampstead and in Northumberland, where he was High Sheriff. The family was of Huguenot merchant extraction, reflecting the old links between the mercantile interests of the Protestant world. The Barings were perhaps the most notable of the trustee families, their German Protestant extraction again illustrating a Protestant con-fraternity of business that was almost as important in London commercial life as the Jewish connection. Thomas Baring, elected in 1839, was the son of Sir Thomas Baring, and the brother of Sir Francis Baring, first Lord Northbrook, and Conservative M.P. for Great Yarmouth and Huntingdonshire. A director of the Bank of England, and of the East and West India Dock Companies, he was chairman of Lloyds for nearly forty years.

Family connection led naturally to the association of particular firms with Morden College: the union of Baring Brothers with Finlay Hodgson and Co. brought two of the Hodgson brothers onto the Board at the College. James Steward Hodgson, the last of the East India Company trustees, summed up the world so many of his predecessors inhabited: he was J.P. and High Sheriff for Surrey, and Lord of the Manor of Haslemere and Godalming. The Heath family, one of whom was a director of the Bank of England, complete the litany of family names among the trustees.

Despite the erosion of a specifically merchant mentality, the consciousness of caste and of the unique identity of the City still continued powerfully among the great merchants in this period. So much is apparent from the close interest of the trustees in their less fortunate fellows in the College, the only one for decayed merchants in the country (a Liverpool Merchants' Guild was started in 1914), though it catered for the gentle poor at large rather than merchants alone).

62

Whether during their visitations or at their regular meetings in the City (at the premises of the different trustees perhaps, or at South Sea House for much of the time), the trustees took a close and scrupulous interest in the moral and religious well-being of the members.[3] This often personal enforcement of the rules – seen especially in their collection of fines – found a parallel in the conduct of their own meetings, where latecomers and absentees were fined.[4] This degree of involvement, much greater than that usually seen in the eighteenth century, was of a piece with their enthusiasm for the expansion of the College and the efficiency of the estate, a policy again in contrast with the last years of the Turkey Company.[5] This concern for the moral rectitude of the members was characteristic of society as a whole at the time, an age of reform in the economic and political as well as the social sphere. State reform of charity was one aspect of this desire to improve society, and it will be considered in due course. Institutional reform, however, was most often a reflection of the desire to improve the individual. Though this desire was most often expressed in what the monied classes wanted to do to the poor, it also took the form of the respectable reforming the laggard in their own ranks, and especially those who had fallen from the grace of prosperity. The history of Morden College offers a chance to see 'improvement' at work within the middle classes. The craze for reform was to be found among the trustees, but it took its most characteristic expression in one man, Henry William Smith, treasurer of Morden College from 1819 to 1872.[6] Smith stamped his presence on the entire history of the College in the nineteenth century.

As was so often the case, Smith competed for the post of treasurer with others who claimed kinship with the founder's family. He in fact shared much in common with the membership over which he ruled. From his father, partner in a merchant house who made his way up the hard way, Smith would have learned something of the mentality which risk produced in merchant life. His own generation was irreproachably successful, his father placing sons in the Church, the Army and Navy, and the Civil Service. Henry William Smith's education was divided between a merchant's office and the University of Leipzig. Smith was aided in his College labours by the chaplain, for much of this period a kind of deputy-treasurer. The chaplain noted cases of illness, deaths, and attendance at religious worship. He had charge of petty matters of discipline[7] – cautioning members and their relatives for instance – and acted as a general arbitrator in the members' affairs. He also imposed minor fines for such matters as sleeping out or getting in through the College windows.

During Smith's tenure of office, however, the conduct of the chaplain was not always to his liking, nor his control over College affairs as absolute as he would have liked. Son followed father as chaplain in 1842 when the Rev. William Marsh junior succeeded the Rev. William Marsh senior. The latter had

previously made further room for his family by appointing his daughter chapel organist. The chaplaincy was kept in the family from 1819 to 1862.[8] While Marsh the elder was not always as correct in his implementation of the trustees' dictates as Smith would have liked,[9] Marsh the younger was undoubtedly lax in the extreme. This is how one member described him in 1848: 'The costume of the Reverend Gentleman is far from the sanctity of his calling and has called forth much comment, it being more the appearance of a Butcher or Birdcatcher than a Clergyman: his skill in shooting larks, breeding and catching Birds and Butterflies is notorious'.[10] Marsh does indeed seem to have kept an aviary in his room, and certainly rented part of his house to boarders. Marsh's answer to the latter charge, brought against him by the trustees, was that his father often had eight or nine boarders in the house.[11] Marsh junior allowed female relatives of members to reside in the College, neglected his religious office, and seems to have given unauthorised permission to absentees.[12]

Not too much store need be set by the words of complaint issuing from Marsh's chief detractor, one William Bourne, who claimed that Marsh had bad debts in the neighbourhood, and a wife of 'somewhat irregular habits' said to visit members in their rooms almost daily.[13] Nonetheless, his wife did go insane in 1859,[14] and Marsh himself brought a kind of mayhem into College life. What Bourne disliked were Marsh's supposed Puseyite leanings.[15] Bourne was in fact a troublesome member, and the trustees did not find against Marsh for sanctioning irreverence to the Church of England. More than this however, what Bourne seems to have disliked most of all was Marsh's ease and familiarity with the members. Because of his failings, rather than despite them, Marsh enjoyed a great popularity among the members. Bourne contrasted Marsh with Smith, 'whose habits entitle and command respect'. It is clear that a good deal of the respect of the members went not to Smith but to Marsh. What Marsh's

Henry William Smith,

College Treasurer, 1819–1872
A notable guardian of the Victorian
moral conscience

College career so clearly reveals is the undercurrent of discontent and opposition to authority that ran through College life so much of the time. It was around the figure of Marsh, who so clearly represented what a 'sober, pious and discreet' member should *not* be, that the limited possibilities in College life for the organisation of this undercurrent of feeling were brought to the surface and given direction and point.

The Rev. John Harbord, who followed Marsh in 1865, was a man much closer to the treasurer's heart. He worked hand in glove with Smith to reform the College, and was very popular with the trustees, whose meetings he often attended. His popularity no doubt owed something to his being the son of a baronet, and, again, a collateral descendent of the founder.[16] The joint effort of Harbord and Smith at moral and spiritual regeneration was to make a considerable impact on the life of both members and servants. Harbord's influence was so great that after Smith's death a 'standing rule' grew up that no one should be admitted without the chaplain's approval. Harbord was well rewarded for his trouble, as were all College chaplains in the nineteenth century. The author of the Charity Commission's revised scheme of college government in 1871, and of the preceding report on the College, Thomas Hare, expressed his misgivings at the privileged financial position of the chaplain, and the office being in large measure an heirloom of those who could show kinship with the founder. The scheme of 1871 moved to remunerate the chaplain on a salaried basis rather than by the now very lucrative rental from the land with which the position had been endowed. The trustees fought hard against the proposal but were forced to give in in 1880. Even so, with a salary fixed at £800 per annum, the rewards of the chaplaincy were not inconsiderable.[17]

No one disagreed with the 1871 scheme as much as the next chaplain, Henry Lansdell, appointed in 1892. His days at the College, to be described in the next chapter, were spent less often in ministration to the members than in avid pursuit of his antiquarian and literary interests, among which was a learned but interminable College History. Lansdell's neglect was so flagrant, except for his loud complaints about the member's behaviour, that he was forced out of office by the trustees. His attitude to the members, by whom he was heartily disliked, was of a piece with his attitude to his parishioners during his term as a junior curate in Greenwich.[18] Greenwich by this time had grown enormously, many of the population, in Lansdell's words, living in 'the utmost poverty and most squalid misery'. Besides his attacks on drink (the usual nineteenth-century clerical bromide) and his Cottage Lectures (the product of his antiquarian daydreams) Lansdell did as little for these people as for the members.

A good idea of the relationship between the servants and the members can be gained from the rules for female servants issued in 1871.[19] These were in part drawn up to prevent the servants making the College their own. Servants or their families were not to occupy the rooms of members nor to use any part of the College as a workroom. Their personal washing was not to be done in the College, and their children were not to visit with them constantly nor run about. The Sabbath was to be kept quietly, chapel attended, and male visitors or relatives were forbidden in the servants' rooms on that day. A ten p.m. curfew was to be rigidly adhered to. It is clear that the rules had hitherto been all but ignored, and that in treating the College as an open house the servants now had to be put in their place. The attempt to do this was made partly in terms of moral reform, and partly in terms of ending the familiarity of members and servants, a condition of things that to the trustees threatened good order and the social position of gentlemen merchants.

The moral order enshrined in the rules was given form by the most characteristic means of organisation in College history, the family. As early as the 1850s the treasurer's wife had taken upon herself the general superintendence of the female servants and nurses.[20] Concern for the female servants in turn devolved upon the College Clerk's wife. This system was reinforced when the Rev. John Harbord took over as chaplain, and Henry William Smith at last found a fellow-spirit. Mrs. Smith and Mrs. Harbord joined forces to oversee the affairs of the women servants and nurses. This kind of paternalistic, familial control, and the mythology that buttressed it, was in fact very characteristic of the age of liberal capitalism, whether in the individual firm,[21] the middle-class household, or within the middle-class family itself.[22] Indeed, contrary to received opinion, it is probable that it was more characteristic of the age of liberalism and individualism than of the society that preceded nineteenth-century industrial and commercial England. The cultivation of home sweet home as a haven from the cruel world outside, and the elaboration of paternalist, familial means of control and influence were certainly

66

The Rev. the Honourable John Harbord,
College Chaplain, 1865–1892
Fellow-spirit of Treasurer Henry Smith

more consciously articulated and implemented in the nineteenth century,[23] as the society that had once given these characteristics at least some vestige of substance slowly disintegrated.

On the limited canvas of Morden College, at least, the patriarchal family as a mode of institutional order was far more in evidence in the nineteenth than at any time in the preceding century other than the very earliest years. Not only did the two leading ladies of Morden College join forces under their respective masters, but Harbord also got his entire family to abstain from drink. The next step in influencing the servants was to enlist the aid of their upper echelon, and Mr. and Mrs. Soyer, the Chapel Clerk-cum-Butler and Matron, were duly enlisted as total abstainers. What is especially interesting about this use of the family is that it was in part established to pre-empt the use of familial sub-contracting as a means of organisation in servant labour. Thus formally similar divisions of labour were in conflict, an interesting example of a kind of conflict that pervaded Victorian society and of which we know next to nothing. Servants' attitudes to their own work, an expression of their wish to treat the College as a home as well as a place of work, thus offered a counter-definition of how work and home should be regarded. The female servants in the College employed their kin (usually their daughters) as chars, for whom they found wages and meals. It was this system that the re-organisation of discipline attacked.

Putting the servants, and members, in their place required, as we have seen, that the familiarity existing between the two should be ended. By the 1871 rules servants were not to take drink or gratuities from members, and there was to be no familiar talk or gossip between the two. Servants were not to sit down in the members' apartments. Three years earlier, the servants orders had been amended so as to make them inform on the failings of the members.[24] The final rule of 1871 summed up the ethos of the approach: servants were enjoined to live in goodwill and harmony as members of one family. This reform of discipline was accompanied by paternalist measures of social provision, again more in evidence then than in the preceding century.

In 1827 the annual pew monies were donated to the servants, supplementing their yearly gratuities at Christmas and Visitation Day.[25] In 1829 money from endowments was invested in consols to provide a Legacy Fund to supplement wages.[26] A year earlier the servants' sleeping quarters were improved and a day room provided.[27] Payments for good conduct and long service were sometimes made, and old and ill servants of long-standing might be provided with pensions and the use of College rooms.[28] The stick as well as the carrot was applied: in 1848 and 1849 two successive College Men, as well as the wife of the first, were expelled for rudeness and drinking.[29] The faithful servant could expect promotion through the hierarchy: in 1877 the College Man and his wife replaced the College Clerk and his wife, the Superintendent of Female Servants. The College Man's Deputy was put in his vacated place.[30] Preferment as well as faithful service could also be the source of reward: in 1835 the new Chapel Clerk was appointed with the support of the East India merchant in whose business house he had worked as a writer and porter.[31]

The registers of applications and members give us a much more detailed picture of the membership in this period than previously.[32] As the following tables make plain the whole range of the merchant community received admittance, though the majority of members could not be numbered among the greatest of the merchant fraternity. The figures here are for the hundred members admitted between 1826 and June 1848.[33]

Information on the trades to which the members were brought up, and in which they failed is also available. Of the hundred members admitted in this period almost half (47) were trained and usually apprenticed in a merchant house. This designation covered clerks, underwriters and sons of merchant fathers. However, details are often vague (e.g. 'West Indies Trade' or 'merchant Business'), and it is difficult to be precise about origins. Nevertheless, it seems probable, given the expense of training and apprenticeship, that the majority so brought up to business were from fairly substantial backgrounds. It was clear that the merchant community was self-recruited to a very considerable degree. The next most important group were factors and wholesale dealers in total 18. It is difficult to segregate some of these from the merchant background proper. There were 10 manufacturers, including two shipbuilders. Only two came from a naval background, and of the 17 others for whom information is available, most were of indeterminate description such as 'fruit trade', 'tobacco trade', or 'wool trade' (though there numbered among them stationer's apprentices, 'superintendents', and 'clerks'). Though these members came from a variety of backgrounds they met their financial fall as merchants, a good many of them

68

Table 1 Eligible Applicants for Morden College

Membership, 1826–1848: Financial Standing

(a)		(b)	
Amount of Annual Transactions[1]		*Amount of Debts when Failed*	
Over £100,000	16	Over £50,000	4
£50–99,000	22	£41–50,000	5
£20–49,000	20	£31–40,000	2
£10–19,000	13	£21–30,000	14
under £10,000	19	£11–20,000	11
No Information	10	£1–10,000	32
		Under £1,000	10
		Other[2]/No Information	22

1. Almost invariably a career maximum figure is entered in the register, thus to some degree exaggerating the scale of business formerly carried on by members. Figures for annual payments to banks are also available, though these are less complete.
2. A number of members were not bankrupted.

describing themselves as 'general merchants' and the others from an enormously wide variety of trades, among which wine merchants were prominent. Some combined trading with manufacturing and wholesale dealing.

The entrance requirements at the College were nevertheless still strict, and to this end questions were asked about the extent, if any, of candidates' shipowning. Merchants had to be *bona fide* trans-maritime merchants, and the sending of goods in consignment was a major criterion for entry. The prohibition on retailing was strong, by the 1881 rules the candidates being explicitly asked whether they kept an inn, hotel, shop, or in any way dealt in retail.[34] Information from the College registers for those not admitted in the 1826–57 period makes it clear that besides age, religion, degree of present prosperity and the other stipulations, inland trading and retailing were major causes of refusal to admit. Nonetheless, by 1881 there was some relaxation of the entry requirements, wholesale dealers then being admitted. The insistence that applicants be of at least ten years' standing in their business, and that they be genuine and not self-inflicted cases of misfortune was still rigidly adhered to.

Between 1695 and 1867 593 members were admitted, and between the latter date and 1972 a further 515. In this period the requirement of Anglican observance was important, candidates having to obtain a certificate from their parish priest stating that they attended worship and the sacrament regularly. Smith, the treasurer, took pains to see that none but Anglicans were admitted, and there are several cases of Wesleyans being refused. As in the eighteenth century a quiet, sober and respectful disposition was looked for. Causes of business failure in the first half of the century ranged through the whole catalogue of mercantile calamity from loss of ships and cargoes to the effects of economic depression.[35] In this period the Napoleonic Wars and their aftermath was a singularly productive cause of disruption for the merchant community, and many went broke as a result of military action and the general economic dislocation. War, and ensuing unsettling peace, were a cause of business failure throughout the whole of the College's history. The single most important cause of failure, however, were the bad debts of customers, and the bad speculations, as well as bad faith, of business partners.

The London and the City connections were always the most powerful in the composition of the membership. A number of members began their careers in provincial settings, especially ports, and a few continued to ply their trade outside the capital. Others spent much of their business careers abroad, and a number of foreign-born merchants were sometimes to be found among the members in this period. But for the great majority London was either the nub of the entire mercantile career or the magnet that drew the provincial immigrant. The provincial 'incomer' was a familiar figure in the eighteenth-century merchant community as well. Members in the 1814–1831 years declared themselves to be 'Citizens of London', City housekeepers and freemen of the livery companies.[36]

Many of the members had failed a good while before being admitted to the College, and in the period between would often have been long exposed to the experience of poverty and loss of station. It is difficult to capture the keenness of this loss. To do so the very high number of merchants who had been apprenticed as merchants and lived most of their lives as such must be borne in mind. What had been lost was thus more a way of life than an occupation, a long experience of friends, customs and connections within an occupational calling that had much in common with a caste or a confraternity. This sense of loss would have been further sharpened by the dropping away of the customary life and fellowship of the livery companies to which so many members belonged. In understanding the reactions of members to life in the College, to the experience of the order of College life and the restitution of a measure of status, the importance of the occupational community of the merchant and of its loss must be constantly present to mind.

The years between failure and admission were often long, hard and bitter. Once considerable merchants ended up as commercial travellers, rent or debt collectors, copiers of legal documents, or in some back street commission business. Most eked out a living with minute pensions, or annuities and gifts from relatives and friends. 'Commission on sales, translating foreign languages, very precarious' is a typical entry in the Registers. In the often long years of penury some members established a niche for themselves by which adversity might be contained: one man admitted in the 1830s had failed long before in the 1790s. During this period he worked as an assistant to a Lloyds' underwriter, also acting as a (self-described) 'arbitrator of differences in the Hide and Skin

70

**The Old East India House
Leadenhall Street 1648 to 1726**

Market' in a City tavern.[37] Men like John Peters were commonplace in the College – elected in 1835, he failed as an Indies trader, failed again as an oil merchant, and sank eventually to the rank of a common seller of coal.[38]

To escape this condition the help of the influential was needed. Applicants had to be supported by letters of recommendation; and the more notable the patron in London commercial, especially mercantile, life the more chance the applicant had of succeeding. Members vied with one another over the length of their petition rolls, on which were inscribed the names of the respectable of the City. This paraphenalia of letters of conduct, petition rolls, and questionnaires ensured the protracted and keen courtship of the mighty by the humble.[39] As indicated in chapter two above, information on members, and decisions on their admittance, would have been a product of the City grapevine, of which the College trustees, the leading business figures of the day, were in so many ways the root and source. The largest single source of information on candidates was the London merchant house itself, and the reputable firm was supplemented by intelligence from banks and from insurance underwriters. When these patrons were M.P.s, Aldermen or J.P.s their support was all the more valuable, as was that of the occasional military man and the much more frequent clergyman. In fact, in wooing the notable a keen interest in Church affairs was always an advantage (this was how John Peters made his mark). Applications and petitions were invariably couched in the most deferential of terms.[40]

Turning again to the tenor of College life, the reforming broom so eagerly wielded by the treasurer Henry William Smith went into action almost immediately on his appointment, when he drew the attention of the trustees to the need for a new set of College rules.[41] He seems to have had some immediate

71

success, noting in 1820 how the old system of donations for good behaviour was now working smoothly.[42] A year later he reported on the great improvement in the members' manners and their respect for him. In 1823 the trustees reported that all was now sweetness and light in the College,[43] though Smith and the trustees were a little precipitate in their complacency. Just as the 1821 rules hardly altered the rigours of the eighteenth-century constitution so what is particularly striking about subsequent changes in the nineteenth-century rules (chiefly in 1844, 1875 and 1881) is how little the régime of the College changed with the passing years. The old moral authoritarianism is there in 1875 for instance, members being forbidden to meddle with College affairs, and encouraged to 'employ themselves in acts of piety and devotion', and not to be 'wandering and mis-spending time in public and disorderly houses'. The system of sanctions was still in force, whether in the form of money fines, suspension from College benefits, or expulsion. Attendance at divine service was mandatory.[44] It is only in the 1890s that a new liberality is apparent. By the 1897 rules members were given up to a month's leave of absence in the year and two weeks at Christmas if desired. The daily curfew was now set at eleven p.m. throughout the year. Around the turn of the century members began to come and go, therefore, with a degree of freedom unparalled in the College's history: the recuperative trip to Folkestone is emblematic of the changed order of things.[45]

For the greater part of the century, however, the College laboured under the imperatives of the Victorian moral conscience, above all as given form in the authority of treasurer Smith. The ambience of Victorian moral improvement informs Smith's whole career: he wrote articles for the popular, educational press, including *Chamber's Journal* and *The Penny Magazine*. Charity was an integral part of the crusade. Like so many middle-class philanthropists of the day he was involved in a bewilderingly large range of charitable and Church committees, doing good to an often bewildered populace. The religious infusion was especially important, many of the Victorian philanthropic laity being clerics *manqué*. Smith was active in the Church Missionary Society and the Church Pastoral Aid Society. He also published a design for the pastoral care of the aged called *The Pilgrim's Staff*, and was secretary of King's College, started by Bishop Blomfield to provide youth with an education in the principles of the Church of England.[46] As we have seen, the East India Company trustees complemented Smith's efforts at the College by their close interest in the moral condition of the members.[47]

Both Smith and the trustees were therefore part of the widespread reforming impulse in early-Victorian Britain. The College's attempt to put its own house in order reflected State reform of charity in the period. Henry Brougham, the foremost advocate of charity reform, was also a major propogandist for popular

72

The later East India House in Leadenhall Street. Plans for the erection of a new East India House were prepared in 1796 by Richard Jupp, Surveyor to the Company and building was commenced in 1797

education and political economy. As a workaday version of Brougham, Smith lent his unflagging support to the 'March of Intellect', and Morden College in this period, as in the preceding one, managed to avoid most of the excesses of similar charitable institutions. The failings unearthed by Brougham and the Charity Commissioners in the first half of the nineteenth century ranged from the 'guzzling' of the charity dinner to land-dealing between trustees, and the slipshod administration and exploitation of charitable institutions and revenues.[48] However, if Smith and the trustees were at one with the *Zeitgeist* of reform, they were also at one with the great contemporary suspicion of the State as the agent of that *Zeitgeist.* Nor was the College completely immune from criticism. Because of this suspicion of the State the College was to be numbered among the vested interests that opposed the Charity Commission – the Church, the Lords, the Law, the City companies and the public schools.

The Charity Commissioner's report on Morden College, written by Daniel Fitch in the 1930s, found that the parsimony of the latter days of the Turkey Company administration had resulted in the College not being properly extended.[49] This failing was however set to right early on in the period of the East India Company. More serious allegations were made in the third major lawsuit in College history, brought by the members against the trustees between 1827 and 1845 at a cost of £5,000. The fact of legal proceedings, and their inordinate length and expense, again illustrate the members' capacity to take a hand in their own destinies in defiance of the dictates of the College authorities.[50] Misconduct was alleged in the treasurer's and chaplain's occupancy of members' rooms, the letting of estate property, and the application of the College income. The Charity Commission found there to be substance in only the first, relatively

73

insignificant charge, though the agitation did increase the amount of the members' pensions.

The Charity Commission was to be a permanent feature in College history, as in the history of all similar institutions, from the early nineteenth century onwards. The Charitable Trusts Act of 1853, tightened up by subsequent legislation in the nineteenth century, established the role of the State in private charity: funds were now to be vested in a Treasurer of Public Charities, later the Official Trustee of Charitable Lands, and in the Official Trustees of Charitable Funds. The original powers of enquiry and examination, advice and assistance, framed in the 1853 Act, were later extended to cover the direct formulation and implementation of schemes of management. Nonetheless, the degree of initiative in policy and administration left in the hands of the trustees of private charities has remained considerable. The hand of the State in College affairs was felt forcefully in the years after 1850: the 1871 scheme of management, fully implemented in the further scheme of 1881, represented with comprehensive emphasis the arrival of the State.[51]

Under the schemes a breach was at last made in the founder's claims upon posterity, preferment to the Mordens' kin not being mentioned in the schemes of management. The treasurer's position was made a full-time one, with an annual stipend of £400. The trustees were given clear guidelines on the running of College and estate affairs, though it was rather in the negative than the positive sense that new departures were made. Nothing was said about Anglican allegiance and sobriety of attitude as criteria for admission, and the stipulation that only merchants could apply was at last relaxed. Perhaps the most important departure, however, was the institution of out-pensions to those in a similar category as the members (and later to their widows and orphans as well).[52] The author of the Charity Commission's report of 1865 on Morden College, William Hare, had suggested these pensions as a more 'humane' system than that of residence, to his mind 'practically a forced seclusion' in celibacy away from the society of friends and relatives.[53] In his choice of the term 'forced seclusion' Hare sums up the régime members had lived under and reacted against for so long. All these developments, especially the institution of out-pensions, were to see the beginning of the transformation of the College into its present form.

Despite these schemes things were always slow to change in institutions such as Morden College, and the members continued to react against the *ancien régime* of College authority in its latter days. As we have seen, discontent sometimes took the organised form of legal action. Unlike the eighteenth century, early nineteenth century changes in the procedures of legal enquiry into charities, as well as the setting up of the Charity Commission itself, meant that such actions stood a better chance of success. Those who had instigated the first lawsuit

74

Shareholders at a meeting in the Court Room at the new East India House as depicted by Thomas Rowlandson, the caricaturist (1756–1827)

against the trustees in the Turkey Company period were summarily dismissed. The litigants of 1827 had more success, though for some there was a price to be paid later. Before that date members were not afraid of asking for increases in their allowance,[54] and after the termination of that long case the threat of recourse to legal action was again made by members. In 1859 a member complained that despite enquiry and reform the chaplain still trespassed upon the members' dignity by having two College apartments. In asking for a more open and responsive form of College government he threatened the College with the wrath of the Charity Commission. This member, S. W. Bishop, and another member taking a similar line in 1878 were both in the end expelled from the College.[55] Opposition to authority was still engaged in at a price.

As in the eighteenth century, the College authorities made their weight felt by means of a semi-monitorial system among the members. The system of paid member-visitors seems to have continued, and to have been supplemented by the paid office of sub-treasurer's assistant.[56] Member-visitors were also put in charge of the library. The six oldest members formed a kind of head-boy cadre: under the Vansittart legacy they enjoyed some financial reward from their standing. Continuity with the previous period was also found in the democracy of the dinner table. In order to move table a member had to have the trustees' permission but also the majority vote of his new and old tables. It was at the separate tables of the Dining Hall that the 'cabal' and the 'confederacy' took root.[57] College life in the period was fairly regularly punctuated by occasions of bad order.

Despite periodic purges of members' and servants' relatives residing in the College,[58] the practice continued, as members attempted to lighten the 'forced seclusion' of their existence.[59] Expulsions, suspensions and warnings for absenteeism, insulting behaviour and 'immorality' were regular occurrences throughout the century.[60] When the trustees acted in accordance with the members' sensitivities as gentlemen merchants a quite opposite reaction was possible: in 1845 the members presented the trustees with a silver inkstand for putting up their allowance.[61] Of course, some members – aged and ill – were especially difficult. Such a one was Charles Eicke.[62] Despite repeated warnings in the late 60s and early 70s Eicke proceeded to foment ill-feeling among his fellows by his bad debts and scandal-mongering. In 1873 Eicke even incited a local publican to write an insulting letter to the chaplain claiming that the members were breaking the excise laws by running their own gin shops. Not surprisingly, the trustees were a little sceptical. Nonetheless, though Eicke was a difficult customer, they moved against him with a real degree of ruthlessness, expelling him despite his abject surrender to them, and the obvious mental suffering the thought of his impending destitution brought to this ill and difficult man.

The case of Thomas Garner Richmond was rather different.[63] He was one of those who instigated the lawsuit of 1827. When the trustees at last acted against him he claimed that he had not been properly informed of the charges against him, and called on the 'Englishman's right' to a fair defence: 'We are not schoolboys now at the age of 73 years' as he says. The trustees seem to have threatened the others engaged in the 1827 lawsuit before moving against Richmond.[64] Richmond did not go gladly and repeatedly entered the College to press his case in the loudest terms, a policeman coming to collect him after one outburst in the chapel. In the end a stipendiary magistrate had to restrain him. We have already noted the chaplaincy of William Marsh junior, and the occasion it offered for spirits like in temper to express their opposition to high-handed authority, especially the authority of H. W. Smith. Marsh's popularity was owed to his easy-going style, and it was around his figure that discontent was given a measure of organisation. As his detractor Bourne described Marsh's rooms, they were '. . . the constant place of call for Bird catchers and people of the lowest classes. Also the rendezvous of persons of the College for concerting Dissension and engendering Dissatisfaction among the Members . . .'.[65] Marsh called on the members throughout the day, taking wine with them and listening to their troubles.

Again as in the eighteenth century, the chief source of disorder was drink. The reason for the Rev. Harbord's personal abstinence crusade was the drunkenness of so many members. Harbord claimed that between 1866 and 1880 nine members were expelled for drunkenness, and that in his time subsequent to this sixteen others had died from drink![66] Whatever the truth of this, drink was rife in the College into the twentieth century.

This was nowhere more clearly in evidence than on the occasion of Founder's Day in 1888. Large amounts were spent on food and drink, the vast menu for the day reminding us that charity dinner 'guzzling' had not died in the early nineteenth century. The consequence of this lavish provision was that two factions among the membership started fighting each other and the day ended in uproar.[67] After this Founder's Day was reformed, the trustees refusing to attend for a good many years afterwards. The members' complaints about the injustice of all this were met by the trustees reiteration of the founder's rule that it was none of the members' business to meddle in College affairs. The upshot of the day was that three members were expelled. Warnings and expulsions for drunkenness and abusive behaviour were frequent in the period, providing ample opportunity for Harbord, and Lansdell who came after him, to exercise their moral zeal.[68] Yet the events of 1888 were rather the curtain descending on the old style of authority and the old disorder than the herald of a new phase of bacchanalia. It is to the stability and harmony that by and large characterised the aldermanic period of College government that we shall now turn.

References for Chapter Five

1. For further biographical information on the East India Company trustees see H. Lansdell, *Princess Aelfrida's Charity* (1911, 1914), chap. LVI.

2. On the London money market see F. Sheppard, *London 1808–1807: The Infernal Wen* (1971), chap. 2, also chap. 5.

3. H. Lansdell, *op. cit.*, chap. LXI, p. 31.

4. Minutes: 9 April, 10 June 1824, for the institution of this practice, carried on with enthusiasm in the East India Company period.

5. Lansdell, *op. cit.*, chap. XLVI.

6. For biographical details of Smith, *ibid.*, chaps. XXXV–VI.

7. A good idea of the chaplain's function can be had from the Leave of Absence Register, 1854 onwards, in Chaplain's Books and Reports/ Register of Services, in Morden College Muniment Room.

8. On the Marsh family, Lansdell, *op. cit.*, chap. LXI.

9. Minutes: 4 March 1837.

10. Minutes: 17 April 1848.

11. *Ibid.*, 5 July 1847; 2 September 1850.

12. *Ibid.*, 23 September; 8 July 1850.

13. *Ibid.*, 17 April; 19 June 1848.

14. *Ibid.*, 14 December 1859.

15. Marsh's Puseyite leanings, as opposed to his personal style, do not seem to have been a cause of his popularity. In line with eighteenth century feeling, religious orthodoxy was a force uniting the whole body of the College. On Marsh using a Puseyite curate and chapel attendances dropping off because of this, cf. William Hay correspondence, 1843–53: Members' Correspondence Bundles, M.C. Muniment Room.

16. On Harbord see Lansdell, chaps. LXVII-III.

17. *Ibid.*, chap. LXVI.

18. *Ibid.*, chap. LXIV.

19. Rules and Orders, Female Servants of Morden College, June 1871, in H. Elphinstone Rivers' Scrapbook, M.C. Muniment Room.

20. Minutes: 4 July 1853, 16 February 1859.

21. P. Joyce, *Work, Society and Politics: The Culture of the Factory in Later Victorian England* (Harvester Press and Rutgers University Press 1980), chaps. 4, 5.

22. E. J. Hobsbawn, *The Age of Capital, 1848–1875* (1977), p. 281.

23. See D. Roberts, *Paternalism in Early Victorian England* (Rutgers University Press, New Brunswick, 1979). Roberts, however, fails to enter into the question of the *response* to paternalist influence and control in any depth. This is the question that, above all others, needs answering. Nor is he aware of the degree to which conscious practice *and* the promptings of cultural *milieu* in the factory North led to a powerful revival of paternalism in the later nineteenth century. See my *Work, Society and Politics, passim.*

24. Minutes: 20 February 1868.

25. Minutes: 15 January, 28 February 1827.

26. *Ibid.*, 21 February 1829.

27. 22 March 1828.

28. 21 February 1826; 18 November 1850; 25 October 1877.

29. 12 July 1847; 17 April 1848; 23 August 1849.

30. *Ibid.*, 25 October 1877.

31. 13 December 1834, 31 January 1835.

32. Registers of Applications and Members, 1827 onwards, M.C. Muniment Room.

33. First Register, 1826–1857; 1826 to applicant no. 274, June 1848. The information available from this source may be supported and supplemented by members letters, forms of application, (1) 1814–31, (11) 1832–43. These are currently being put in order by the College Archivist.

34. 1881 Rules and Orders, H. E. Rivers' Scrapbook, Muniment Room.

35. Causes of failure are given in the Registers of Applications and Members.

36. Applications for membership, MSS letter bundles, 1814–31; M.C. Muniment Room.

37. First Register of Applications and Members, no. 45.

38. Members Letter Bundles, 1822–1857, John Peters.

39. For this paraphenalia see Applications for membership, MSS letter bundles, 1814–1843.

40. Cf. Completed Application Forms, 1801–10.

41. Minutes: 11 October 1820.

42. Minutes: 24 June 1820.

43. Minutes: 23 June 1821, 28 January 1823.

44. Rules and Orders, 1844, 1875, 1881.

45. Rules and Orders, 1897; Leave of Absence Register 1890–1912.

46. On Smith see H. Lansdell, *op. cit.*, chaps. XXXV–VI.

47. See also *ibid.*, chap. LXI.

48. On nineteenth century charity reform see D. Owen, *English Philanthropy 1660–1960* (1965), chaps. VII, XI, also chap. X.

49. Thirty Second Report of Charity Commissioners, *Parliamentary Papers* 1837–8, XXVI (140), pp. 842–862.

50. On the lawsuit see Minutes: 17 March 1832, 12 November 1840, 17 March 1843; also Lansdell, chaps. XLI–II, XLIV.

51. Schemes of Management, copies of which are lodged with the Central Registrar of Charities, the Charity Commission: 1871, 1881, 1890, 1896, 1951(2), 1958, 1962, 1974, 1975.

52. Lansdell, chap. LXV.

53. 'Correspondence between the Treasury . . . etc.', *P.P.* 1865, XLI (382), p. 176.

54. Miscellaneous correspondence, re. members, 1822–1857: esp. March 1824, May 1827. As well as references in note 50 above, on the 1827 lawsuit, see also Minutes: November 1833, March 1834.

55. Minutes: 14 December 1859, also S. W. Bishop letter bundle; Minutes: 5 September 1878.

56. Minutes: 22 March 1828.

57. Miscellaneous correspondence re. members, 1822–1857: William May letter bundle, 1843–53, esp. 21 May 1844. For changes in the dinner system, 21 May 1874, 3 November 1975.

58. Minutes: 2 August, 15 November 1832.

59. Minutes: 16 September 1850, 8 July 1874.

60. E.g., Minutes: 8 September 1832; 31 January 1835; 20 February 1868; 1 February 1872; Minutes for 1879.

61. Minutes: 19 November 1845.

62. Miscellaneous correspondence, re. members, expulsions, etc.: C. Eicke bundle; see also Minutes: 17 July, 19 June 1867, 14 August 1873.

63. Miscellaneous correspondence re. members: T. G. Richmond bundle; also Minutes: 17, 20 June, 1 August 1844.

64. Minutes: 7 January 1841.

65. Minutes: 17 April 1848.

66. Lonsdell, *op. cit.*, chap. LXVII.

67. *Ibid.*, chap. LXVIII, also Minutes: 19 July 1888, 20 June, 23 October 1890.

68. Minutes: 13 February 1823; 1837; 6 February 1843; 28 August 1849; 20 February 1868; 1875, etc.

Sir Andrew Lusk, M.P.
Chairman of the Trustees, 1889–1896
Self-made man and defender of City interests

Reproduced from *Vanity Fair*, October 1871

CHAPTER SIX

The World of Morden College III –
The City Aldermen Period,
1884 to the Present

The ending of the East India Company in 1874 did not see the severance of the East India Company trustees from College affairs. It took a court case in 1880 to accomplish this.[1] The East India Company trustees' retention of their interest was a pretension to former glory that the City would not stand for, and twenty-six aldermanic litigants entered the lists against the old trustees. The pride of the City was stung, especially as the institution in question had for so long been on especially clear reflection of the self-consciousness of the City. The prime-mover among the City aldermen was Sir Andrew Lusk, a self-made Scot and Presbyterian. A shipowner and ship-stores dealer, Lusk was an illustration of the City's capacity for absorbing new wealth. The new wealth of self-made men nevertheless brought with it some resistance to traditions of vested interest, especially when, as with the East India Company and Morden College, the shadow of a shadow persisted in its privilege. It was Lusk who raised the matter of the trusteeship on the floor of the House, in 1878,[2] after the formal expiry of an institution that had for long been but a dull reflection of the East India Company of former times.

After Lusk became the chairman of the trustees in 1885 the Court of Aldermen of the City of London gained complete control. In 1895 the final four East India Company trustees resigned.[3] Whatever Lusk's motives, religious and political orthodoxy was the order of the day in the first few decades of the City Aldermen. The exceptions were Sir William Lawrence, the Unitarian, Liberal banker, and Sir Robert Nicholas Fowler, also a banker, though a Quaker turned Anglican, and a Liberal turned Tory. The remainder of the seventeen trustees up to 1914 were Conservative and Anglican.[4] Almost all of these trustees, and those that followed them in the twentieth century, were Lord Mayors. City office, and involvement in Morden College, were two aspects of the immersion of new wealth in the corporate life of the City, for, as the exclusive grip of the mercantile-financial interest weakened, builders, auctioneers and estate agents, and hoteliers and wholesale grocers made their appearance in City government and City philanthropy. The Morden College Board numbered these interests among its trustees in the period. That the City opened up to them and they to the Anglican Church and the Conservative party is testimony to the growing cultural unity of the British business classes at the turn of the present century. New sources of wealth merged with old and old with new. Sir John Whittaker Ellis, elected a trustee in 1907, diversified his auctioneer and estate agent business as chairman of the Alliance Bank and Sir Alfred Newton, a merchant and shipowner elected in 1910, was chairman of Harrods and D. H. Evans. These trends were to be fully worked out in the course of the twentieth century. The livery companies played a similar role to that of City government and charitable institutions in cementing the unity of diverse and new interests. All the trustees, into the present, were closely involved with the companies, many with several of them. Sir Robert Fowler was typical with his involvement in the Spectacle Makers, the Loriners and the Salters.

Thus the institutional and ceremonial world of the City accommodated diversity, not that these new entrants to the field were not already schooled in acceptable behaviour, religion and politics. Self-made men of the rags-to-riches kind were few and far between, and a public school and Oxbridge education was the hallmark of the builders and grocers in this period, just as the financiers and merchants. City government, and involvement in the companies and adopted philanthropic institutions of the City has continued to be the signature of acceptance and respectability in high City society into the present. The City involved itself in the substance as well as the ritual of power. In the period before 1914 almost all the trustees were Conservative MPs, sometimes for London but more usually for the safe further-flung seats their money and standing merited. This degree of political involvement has been less characteristic of the period after 1914, though subsequent trustees have held prominent positions in London's social and economic life, positions that complemented their involvement in the corporate life of the City. Before 1914 trustees were involved with the Metropolitan Board of Works, the Thames Conservancy Board, the London County Council, the School Board and the Docks, and their successors have occupied similar strategic positions in London life. The connection between the College and the City was given overt expression when the trustees began meeting at the Guildhall in the 1890s, a practice continued until 1941 when it was bombed. Thereafter, meetings were held at the Mansion House for a time.[5] Royal favour has further increased the standing of trusteeships in the present century. Queen Mary made a private visit to the College in 1937,[6] and the present Queen visited in 1971 to open Cullum Welch Court the new nursing centre.

Turning to the management of College affairs, the division of labour between treasurer and chaplain apparent after the death of Henry William Smith in 1872 was continued during the chaplaincy of the Rev. Henry Lansdell (1892–1912).

82

Like the Rev. Harbord before him, Lansdell had a large degree of responsibility for selecting and interviewing candidates for admission. In this task he afforded himself the most 'scientific' method of ascertaining the respectable and deserving, going to the Charity Organisation Society to see how the job could best be done.[7] The separation of the 'business' from the personal side of management was a characteristic of the College in the twentieth century. In 1905 a treasurer was appointed without College accommodation for the first time.[8] In 1945 the management of the members' affairs was further separated from estate and College business by the appointment of a warden. This trend to a separation of powers, and to the augmentation of the chaplain's authority, was however reversed in 1953 when the new system of dual control was ended, and the Clerk to the Trustees, the modern equivalent of treasurer, again resumed responsibility for College and staff management.[9]

Despite the increase in the chaplain's influence towards the end of the nineteenth century the trustees' say in the running of the members' affairs was as final as it had always been. Indeed, in the present century, trustee control of the chaplain's powers in the interest of the members represents one of the most important changes in the long history of the members' experience of College life. The ending of the old tension between members and management meant the replacement of a rigorously conceived and enforced system of discipline by one much more responsive, indulgent and humane. Some of the reasons for this will be discussed later when the membership is considered. It is a process clearly at work in the religious affairs of the College as well.

In 1895 the members declared themselves not to be 'in love and charity' with Henry Lansdell, and asked to receive communion outside the College. At this time Lansdell enforced twice-daily religious attendance on a Sunday (morning and evening) and suspended members on his own initiative.[10] Though the trustees were sympathetic to the members' complaints, the situation simmered away until in 1911 twenty-eight members signed a memorial against Lansdell. Whereas in the previous century the trustees would have supported the chaplain and castigated the members now they told Lansdell to resign.[11] Part of the reason for the growing tolerance in College affairs was in fact the declining hold of religion in English life, but still more the waning of the sectarian ardour that invested nineteenth-century Anglicanism in general and College religion in particular. Towards the end of his tenure Lansdell was told not to enquire too closely into the religious tenets of the members.[12] The Charity Commission management schemes of 1881 and 1890 did not stipulate that the members should be Anglican, and though the trustees continued with the requirement it was interpreted with increasing liberality. In 1931 a chaplain was again forced to resign because his rigid Anglicanism had antagonised the members.[13] The marked improvement in the social and religious life of the College noted in the early years of the next chaplain's time has continued to inform College history.[14]

In small and introspective institutions like Morden College the paternalism of the nineteenth century carried over powerfully into the present century, despite the increasing influence of the State. This continuity is apparent in the way College servants were treated, though as usual it was long and faithful servants who tended to receive most of the benefits. These were handed out on an *ad hoc* basis, such as in funeral expenses and retirement doles,[15] though by 1910 or so retirement allowances were mentioned formally among the official 'Duties and Emoluments' of Servants.[16] At this time each servant had the care of six members, and the aid of a charwoman if she looked after more. A Superannuation Scheme for staff was organised in 1929 and a retirement pension scheme in 1948.[17] Despite this continuation of paternalistic concern, in line with wider social change in the twentieth century, the 'household' organisation of College life has given way to the looser, more functional institutional forms characteristic of other such charitable bodies. The change is reflected most of all in the College servants no longer living in the College. Nonetheless, the idea of the College as a community of like-experienced equals is a lively one in the present.

The composition of the College membership in the twentieth century has been greatly different from that in previous periods. As the College minutes reported the reflections of the Chairman of the Trustees on the question of admission in 1920: 'He further referred to the practical non-existence of, so far as the trustees had been able to discern, a class of "decayed merchants" . . .'.[18] The trustees at this time also reiterated a desire to admit Army and Navy officers as members in their wish to make the College serve the needs of a changed society. To this end the Charity Commission was often rather less than helpful, and it is ironic that it was the institutionalised expression of nineteenth-century reform, the Commission itself, rather than the object of that reform that most wished to preserve the *status quo* by sticking to the letter of the founder's wishes. The spirit of reform was long exhausted and in its place settled a spirit of bureaucratic caution. After a delay of five years the Charity Commission reported in 1925 that it was undesirable that the trustees proceed with an extension of the class to be admitted.[19]

This was their finding even though their own schemes of 1871 and later had defined the terms of entry in a more flexible way.[20] In 1931 it was decided by the trustees that directors of limited companies be admitted, though the Charity Commission laid down stringent terms including a capital stake in the business (share or debenture holders were debarred), and an involvement of at least ten years.[21] On these grounds brokers were not considered eligible in 1933,[22] and as late as 1951 the Charity Commission resisted change in the terms of entry.[23] A year before this a change in this attitude had been made when the trustees decided that their new cottage homes should be open to officers of the merchant marine, the professional classes in general, those in any way engaged in commerce, and – after a resistance of centuries – those in retail trade.[24] This wider definition of the admissible characterises the College membership in the present day as well, the new scheme of 1957 stipulating that those having direction or management in business, and those having ventured experience as well as capital in a trade or profession should be admitted.[25] With this change in the social character of the membership the old tensions that had marked College life were ended. With a wider range of membership, the common lot of the decayed merchant, eager to assert his station as a gentleman, was no longer a focal point for discontent and conflict in College life. With the change in the social composition of the trustees, as well, the degree of conflict within the mercantile community long reflected in College affairs – the ill-feeling between the greater and the lesser in the merchant fraternity – itself ceased to play its former role. College days in the twentieth century were placid and uneventful in comparison with the difficulties of former years, and the lot of the College member was a contented one.

If the notion of the 'gentleman' itself lost some force in the twentieth century, then the members were still drawn from areas of society with a claim to special standing. The amount of pride invested in the notion of the gentleman in the twentieth century certainly lessened as the hold of rank loosened, and became diversified in other forms of customary observance, and this in itself contributed to the equability of College life. But, as in previous periods of College history, the claim to special standing was supported by special provision of amenities and care.

The old system of personal vetting continued into the twentieth century. The standing of a candidate's referees was a matter of importance even after the Second World War.[26] In 1944 a booklet on the College was issued and circulated among 'prominent persons' as a means of getting the 'suitable' to apply.[27] The dominant direction of change, however, as among all charities, was away from 'unofficial', personal contact and towards the bureaucratic, institutionalised organisation of admittance. In the 1920s, in trying to open their doors to a wider range of applicants, the trustees feared that they would be snowed under by applicants, about whom the old system of intelligence would be able to tell very little. One answer to the problem was to suggest that the War Office and Admiralty should vet suitable officers and gentlemen for entry.[28] A later answer was to employ an organisation called the Family Welfare Association to interview candidates from outside the London region. For twenty years before the 1950s this body had seen to it that the deserving who were to be admitted were to be of the right social standing.[29]

The out-pensioners, after 1871, reflected most clearly the changed character of those admitted. Around the turn of the century men such as factory managers, manufacturers and wholesale dealers were representative of the enlarged range

1

2

5

Recent Chairmen
of the Trustees

1946
to the present time

3

4

ALDERMAN LORD BROADBRIDGE
Lord Mayor 1936–1937 *Chairman 1946–1952*

ALDERMAN SIR FRANK ALEXANDER, BT
Lord Mayor 1944–1945 *Chairman 1952–1959*

ALDERMAN SIR FRANK NEWSON-SMITH, BT
Lord Mayor 1943–1944 *Acting Chairman 1959–1962*

ALDERMAN SIR FREDERICK WELLS, BT
Lord Mayor 1947–1948 *Chairman 1962–1966*

ALDERMAN SIR CULLUM WELCH, BT
Lord Mayor 1956–1957 *Chairman 1966–1979*

ALDERMAN SIR RALPH PERRING, BT
Lord Mayor 1962–1963 *Chairman 1979–*

6

of those cared for,[30] a range that was widened still further in the twenties and thirties.[31] The net was cast further than London and wider than Anglican observance alone. As with the merchant membership of the College itself in the nineteenth century, the failed businesses of pensioners ranged widely between the small and the sometimes very substantial. Again, like the members, out-pensioners had often fallen from grace years before a pension was granted, during which time a living might be eked out on the sale of a man's personal effects, a small pension from the Goldsmiths' Company, help from the 'Stock-brokers' Society', or the long-familiar avenues of agency work, travelling on commission, and help from family and friends. Livery company pensions might be supplemented by small amounts from such as the Baltic Benevolent Fund, the Masonic Grant, and small trust monies. One applicant in 1939 ran a small tobacconist's shop after having owned a firm with an annual turnover of £383,000. Others were reduced to taking in paying guests, or to absolute penury. Though the criteria for an out-pension were quite strict – in 1939 a £100 annual income and a house worth £700 debarred an applicant from a pension – none-theless, by adding a College pension of £50 per annum to the various resources of the institutions of middle-class self-help a degree of standing superior to that of the working poor could be secured.

The first two decades of the City Aldermen's period of trusteeship witnessed the last expressions of the discontent and disorder that had for so long been a feature of College life. Drink was still the major problem in the 1890's, though the situation was no doubt a little exaggerated by chaplain Lansdell, who in the fervour of his temperance crusade claimed that the problem haunted him day and night. In 1896 he wrote a pamphlet on the subject and sent it to the trustees.[32] Nonetheless, the trustees' minutes do indicate that arriving in the College drunk was still a fairly commonplace event in the 1890s. So too, in the 1880s, was the kind of behaviour associated with drink. In 1887 a man was expelled for swearing, though – a sign of more tolerant times – he was given an out-pension of £80 a year.[33] Out-pensioners had every occasion to enjoy their pensions as they saw fit. In 1890 one out-pensioner had led such a riotous life in the pubs of Farnborough and Guildford that his neighbours burnt him in effigy![34] His out-pension was duly suspended. Members at this time could still be refused all College benefits for a month as punishment.

The heavy hand of authority was felt after the fracas at Visitation Day in 1888. As we have seen, the trustees greatly resented the members' consequent representations to them as a trespass upon their sole right to order College affairs. Those held responsible for the day were expelled, though again with the concession of a pension.[35] However, the members were not afraid to stand by their rights, and made the occasion of the College bi-centenary in 1895 the pretext for a claim to an increase in their allowance.[36] Discontent had been building up in the 1880s, and in 1887 objections to the administration of the College appeared in the *St. Stephen's Review.*[37] Only a small number of members seem however to have been involved in this agitation, one Frederick Heyn in particular being active in complaining about trustee favouritism and other irregularities.[38] That so few were involved is evidence of the changed climate of things, as is the outcome of the move made by a few members in 1895 to disestablish the College and divert funds into out-pensions only.[39] Despite claims to majority support, at a meeting called in 1897 only eight members attended, and six of these were against disestablishment. Those visited in their rooms were similarly against the move.[40]

We have noted a number of reasons for this transformation from tension and conflict to harmony, order and a new degree of responsiveness on the part of the College authorities. This improvement is given the most striking expression in the decline of instances of drunken and disorderly behaviour after the 1890s.[41] The period between the 1890s and 1914 also saw a much less frequent recourse to the ultimate sanction of expulsion. The person of Henry Lansdell, whose term as chaplain also covered these years, represented the last days of the Victorian reforming zeal that had so much imbued and disrupted the experience of the members. It is thus in those years prior to the First World War that the College entered the modern phase of its development, a phase strikingly different from the long period that went before. Of course, this change was a reflection of larger changes in society, some of which we have mentioned. To changes in the social character of the members and trustees (and to the attitudes of both), should be added such developments as the declining hold of religion, but especially of the old sectarian Anglicanism of the nineteenth century. Many of these changes, in turn, such as the opening out of the 'forced seclusion' so long suffered by the members, are to be ascribed to the changed mental climate of the twentieth century, in which by comparison with Victorian attitudes a good deal of the stigma of poverty, if not always the stigma of age, has been removed. State provision for the poor and aged as of right has replaced private charity's judgement on the degree of deservingness among the prospective recipients. These changes, accelerated by two world wars, have found direct expression in the history of the College.

Nonetheless, a seventeenth-century foundation with such a history as Morden College is a striking survival in the present. And it has carried a good deal of its past character into the present century in the form of a paternalistic attitude to members and tenants. In 1932 a temporary chaplain at Morden College, Farrar Ransom, reported to the trustees that his work at the College reminded him of nothing more than his time as Sunday chaplain on a great Suffolk estate, where '. . . no man, woman or child, on the Estate, need starve if willing to work.'[42] The comparison of the landed estate and Morden College is an instructive one, as are

Broadbridge Close

Opened in 1951 and named after the late Alderman The Rt Hon. Lord Broadbridge, K.C.V.O. The thirty-two flats for married couples are built round a central lawn

Alexander Court

Named after the late Alderman Sir Frank Alexander, Bt., was opened in 1957. The twelve flats provide accommodation for married couples

Wells Court

Named after Alderman Sir Frederick Wells, Bt., was opened in 1966 by H.R.H. Princess Marina, Duchess of Kent. The building provides accommodation for twenty-five residents, sixteen of whom receive domestic and light nursing care

the words chosen to express the comparison: they sum up so clearly the moral ambiguity of paternalism. In 1935 the chaplain and treasurer held an 'At-Home' for the out-pensioners,[43] and from the 1930s onwards the break between the old order and the new becomes increasingly apparent. If paternalism continued it was much less dictatorial and much more responsive than in previous centuries. This is apparent in the trustees' decision of 1956 that in line with 'modern thought' members and out-pensioners should be allowed to pursue an occupation outside the College.[44] This was hardly in line with the founder's wishes, even if the trustees at the time thought it was.

The experience of two world wars did something to cement a new understanding in College affairs. In the first, for example, members volunteered to do the work of enlisted and conscript servants.[45] In the second, despite the College being close to riverside areas of concentrated German bombing (the College was hit and much College property in the vicinity was destroyed), only eleven members decided to evacuate themselves.[46] War unified management and servants also. Servants who either volunteered or were conscripted in the 1914–1918 War were given special allowances as a consequence.[47] Nonetheless, war emboldened people as much as it fostered a spirit of togetherness. Departure for war increased the work load of those left behind and there was considerable ill-feeling among the servants in 1917 until wages were increased.[48] Similarly, returned College servants in 1919 were not slow to ask for wage increases that were duly forthcoming.[49]

The College itself worked to complement the activities of its enlisted servants by contributing to the war effort. In the Great War room was made in College property for Belgian and French refugees, and homeless Greenwich people were similarly housed.[50] The College grounds were used to entertain American soldiers, and permission was given to members to work for the war effort outside the College.[51] At the start of the Second World War the trustees resisted the idea of the College being commandeered in the course of the emergency, thereby expressing their solidarity with the members who had decided to stay on despite the danger. All this represented a continuation of that opening out of the College from its pre-1900 seclusion that has been so marked a feature in the present century. More than at any time in its history Morden College is now a part of the community in which it lies.

The enormous improvement in twentieth-century College life has been as much due to physical improvements in the provision made for members as to any other single cause. Around the turn of the century flush-W.C.'s, electric light and bathrooms did much to humanize the harder existence of earlier days.[52] A new billiards room (1906), Recreation Room (1922), and the installation of radio, telephone and television (the Bush 'Big Picture' set in 1949) worked towards a similar end. A shop was opened in 1954, a workshop in 1971,

and a clubroom and bar in 1973[53]. Improved medical provision was perhaps the major element softening the experience of College life. In 1897 the Medical Officer was asked to give regular reports on the members' health, and to make suggestions about health care.[54] Considerably enlarged medical care was instituted in the 1930s,[55] a development that culminated in the opening of Cullum Welch Court by Her Majesty the Queen on 3rd November 1971. Named after the Chairman of the Trustees at the time of the opening, Colonel Sir Cullum Welch, Bt., O.B.E., M.C., the new medical centre provided accommodation and full nursing care for thirty-eight beneficiaries, men and women.

The most far-reaching change has been the provision of accommodation for old people outside the College itself, though usually in its immediate environs.[56] The number of beneficiaries provided with accommodation has risen from forty-two men in 1945 to upwards of two hundred men and women in 1980. Accommodation includes flats for married couples, flatlets for women, and a specially designed home for those in need of domestic and light nursing care, the work of which complements Cullum Welch Court. Each of the separate developments has been named after the Chairman of the day, with the exception of Montague Graham Court, named after the then Clerk to the Trustees.

Broadbridge Close, opened in 1951 and named after the late Alderman The Rt. Hon. Lord Broadbridge, K.C.V.O., has thirty-two flats for married couples. The flats are arranged on the ground and first floors and look out onto a centre lawn. There is also a community hall for social and other activities, including billiards and snooker. Alexander Court, named after the late Alderman Sir Frank Alexander, Bt., was opened in 1957, and has twelve flats for married couples. Alderman Sir Frederick Wells, Bt., has given his name to Wells Court. Opened in 1966, accommodation is provided for twenty-five residents, sixteen of whom receive domestic and light nursing care. Since 1958 the Trustees have

92

purchased and furnished three houses in Blackheath as flatlets for elderly women who look after themselves domestically. In 1972 a further house was donated by Mr A. R. Martin to the Trustees and converted in the following year. Each house has accommodation for at least seven residents. Montague Graham Court was opened in 1976 and is comprised of three blocks of flats providing accommodation for fifteen elderly women, a Chaplain and a Surveyor. Due to the growth in the number of buildings it is now considered that the Surveyor should be resident within the precincts of the College.

The effort involved in the expansion and extension of the College has been recognised in the appointment of the then Clerk to the Trustees, Mr Montague S. Graham, as a Member of the Most Excellent Order of the British Empire, the first honours award to be made to an officer of the College. The College Surveyor, Mr Kenneth B. Leverton, F.R.I.C.S., was similarly honoured in 1976, and in the June of that year the Queen granted her patronage to the College. Both of the aforementioned officers held senior appointments for upwards of thirty years, the present Clerk, Mr Arthur A. Snashall, being appointed in 1976 following Mr Graham's retirement. Robert V. Chadwick, F.R.I.C.S., was appointed Surveyor in 1980 upon Mr Leverton's retirement, followed by the latter's new appointment as the Trustees' consultant. Mr Snashall and Mr Chadwick were first engaged by the Trustees in 1946. This length of service is typical of the close involvement of many of the College employees in the running of College affairs and the care of the members, and it is to these as well as the officers and Trustees that the present tranquillity of College life is due.

References for Chapter Six

1. 'The Attorney General versus Thomas M. Weguelin and Others', bound copy of proceedings in Morden College Muniment Room; also report of trial in *The Times*, 17 February 1880, p. 4.

2. On Lusk see H. Lansdell, *Princess Aelfrida's Charity* (1911, 1914), chap. LXXII.

3. *Ibid.*, chaps. LXX, LXXI.

4. On the trustees to 1914, *Ibid.*, chaps. LXXII–III.

5. Minutes: 23 January 1941.

6. Minutes: 4 February, 8 April, 4 November 1937.

7. See his own account, H. Lansdell, *op. cit.*, chap. LXXX.

8. Minutes: 6 July 1905.

9. Minutes: 14 October 1953.

10. *Ibid.*, 3 May 1894, 20 June 1895.

11. *Ibid.*, 2 May 1911.

12. Minutes: 2 February 1911.

13. Minutes: 8 October 1931, see also 21 January 1931.

14. 25 January 1934, 13 June 1935.

15. 4 January 1906, 6 December 1910; see also Minutes: 10 December 1930, 11 December 1942.

16. 'Duties and Emoluments of Servants' (1910?), in MSS. Volume, Morden College Servants and Nurses, in Muniment Room.

17. Minutes: 14 November 1929, 18 October 1948.

18. Minutes: 2 February 1920.

19. Minutes: 7 May 1925.

20. Minutes: Charity Commission Letter to Morden College – 28 April 1931.

21. Minutes: 14 May, 9 July 1931.

22. Minutes: Charity Commission Letter to Morden College – 21 March 1933.

23. Minutes: 12 January 1951.

24. Minutes: 20 September 1950.

25. *Ibid.* 30 July 1957, 6 March 1958. Orders sealed by the Charity Commissioners and dated 7 February 1958 and 19 July 1960 enabled the Trustees to admit as inmates and pensioners those holding positions of management or direction in commerce, or in connection with the Merchant Navy, their other qualifications being the same as hitherto. These orders were re-enacted by a more comprehensive Official Scheme sealed on 6 November 1962, which provides for men who have attained rank or position of substantial authority in their employment, business or profession.

26. Register of Applications, 1947–1954.

27. Minutes: 15 April 1944.

28. Minutes: 2 December 1920.

29. Minutes: 12 January 1951, 11 May 1951.

30. Register of Applications, Members and Out-Pensioners: 1885–1896; 1896–1909.

31. Copies of Applications of Residents and Out-Pensioners, 1928–1932.

32. H. Lansdell, *op. cit.*, chap. LXXXIV.

33. Minutes: 6 October 1887.

34. *Ibid.*, 1 May 1890.

35. See above.

36. Lansdell, *op. cit.*, chap. LXXXIII.

37. Minutes: 1 December 1887.

38. Minutes: 8 January 1889, 20 June 1890.

39. *Ibid.*, 31 October, 17 December 1895; 12 November 1896; see also, for the trustees' dealings with the Charity Commission on the matter, Minutes: 4 October 1900 to December 1900; also May 1902, 1903, May 1917.

40. 7 January 1897.

41. For isolated cases see Minutes: 19 October 1906, 7 October 1915.

42. Leave Book 1931, F. Ransom/Trustees, 29 February 1932.

43. Minutes: 13 June 1935.

44. 1 September 1956.

45. Minutes: 12 November 1916.

46. Minutes: 22 September 1939, 19 July 1940; on the bombing, *ibid.*, and 13 October 1944.

47. Minutes: 1 October 1914; see also 1 June 1916, 2 November 1916, etc.

48. *Ibid.*, 4 October 1917.

49. *Ibid.*, 6 December 1919.

50. 1 October 1914, 1 February 1917.

51. Minutes: 6 June 1918; 3 January 1918.

52. Minutes: 3 May 1904, also 1905 Minutes.

53. Minutes: But see 17 June 1946, 9 May 1947.

54. *Ibid.*, 4 February 1897.

55. 9 June 1932; see also 5 October 1937, 29 March 1946.

56. See above, pp. 37–8.

Sir Christopher Wren
1632–1723
From the painting by Sir Godfrey Kneller

A Note on the
Architecture of Morden College

Those interested in the architecture of the College will find it exhaustively discussed in the profusely-illustrated, T. Frank Green, *Morden College, Blackheath, Being the Tenth Monograph of the London Survey Committee* (1916). The present brief account of collegiate architecture and the College may be supplemented by the illustrations in this volume as well as by Green's work.

The essential element in collegiate architecture is the siting of institutional buildings (apartments, hall, kitchen, chapel, etc.) around a central quadrangle. The collegiate tradition derived from the architectural design of the mediaeval monastery, though the design of the first hospitals owed more to the mediaeval church than the mediaeval monastery. Rather than the courtyard plan, the large, aisled hall or dormitory for the sick corresponded to the shape of a church itself, with a chapel at the east end occupying the position of the chancel, and the beds and cubicles the place of the aisles. With the growth of endowments for the aged as well as for the infirm, and therefore of permanent lodging, the quadrangle came into its own as the basic feature of almshouse architecture.

Mediaeval almshouses of this type make their appearance in the first half of the fifteenth century, though it was not until the course of the Reformation that the infirmary type ceded primacy to the collegiate design. Nonetheless, in Tudor and Stuart England, hospital architecture continued to amalgamate older mediaeval characteristics with the new canons of Renaissance architecture. There also continued to be considerable variety within the categories of 'quadrangular' and 'collegiate', almshouses often taking the form of fragmented groups of houses around a square, central area (usually when the houses were not large enough to be built in an enclosed form). The late Renaissance infusion of classicism saw the collegiate design in turn giving way to assemblages of dwellings in one block and to groupings of buildings other than the quadrangular one. The quadrangular tradition persisted in Wren's three-sided Chelsea Hospital, and took its classic, enclosed form in Bromley College (1666), Trinity Hospital, Deptford (1670), and Wren's Morden College (1695). Though there were deviations from Wren's design in the original building, most of all in the omission of a row of dormer windows, Morden College represents one of Wren's finest achievements, and one of the most perfectly realised examples of collegiate architecture.

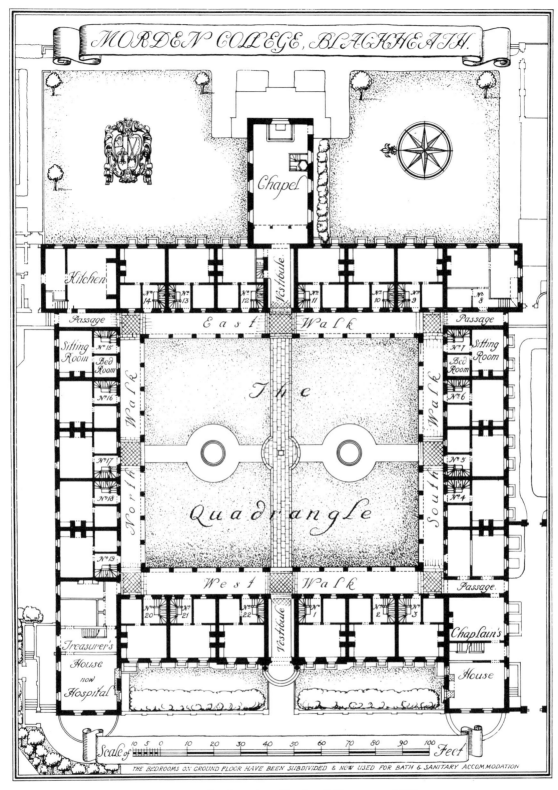

THE BEDROOMS ON GROUND FLOOR HAVE BEEN SUBDIVIDED & NOW USED FOR BATH & SANITARY ACCOMMODATION

Plan of the Quadrangle at Morden College, *circa* **1930**

Reproduced by courtesy of the Royal Commission of Historical Monuments (England)

The College plan consists of a quadrangle of about one-hundred by eighty feet, around which, on the ground floor, runs a covered walk beneath the upper rooms, which are supported by a colonnade. The main entrance is on the west side, immediately opposite the chapel with its vestibule. What were the chaplain's and treasurer's rooms are projections from the main line of the building on the principal, west front. The kitchens and recreation room form the corresponding wings on the east front. The servants' quarters were above the kitchens. The quadrangle is entered by a vestibule on the west front, and two-panelled doors in turn lead from the stone-paved piazza to the members' apartments, which consist of bedrooms and sitting-rooms. The chapel is lit by three windows on each side and a semi-circular-headed window at the east end. The reredos is of richly carved oak, the central portion rising to a height of eighteen feet. Above the two circular-headed panels that form the central portion the arms of William and Mary are enclosed in a cleft pediment. The panels on either side of the central portion of the reredos are inscribed with the Lord's Prayer and the Creed, and surmounting these panels are set the arms of the Morden and Brand families. At the west end of the chapel is a gallery with panelled front supported by square pilasters, with panels filled with carving. The principal additions to the College are the new dining hall (1844), the Kelsall Library (1860) and the billiards room (1906), now the muniment room, replacing the old muniment room (built as the treasurer's office in 1892). The adjacent College grounds were formed in 1851.

The West front of the College is emphasised by two moderately projecting wings with hooded porches. In the pediment in two niches high above the main entrance are two statues of Sir John and his Lady

The central Quadrangle measures 100 feet by 80 feet and presents a very beautiful and peaceful aspect, with its quartered lawns and flower beds

The Chapel interior. The arms over the reredos are those of King William the Third in whose reign the Chapel was completed. Sir John and Lady Morden are buried in the crypt below the chancel

APPENDIX TWO

A Note on Sources

The note apparatus at the end of each chapter gives an adequate notion of the range of material contained in the Morden College archive. The best guide to the College muniments is *Report on the Morden College Muniments*, prepared by A. R. Martin, F.S.A., May 1949. Only a brief description of the very wide range of archival material is possible here. Potentially the richest source of information on the members are the members' letter bundles, manuscript applications, testimonials, etc.; at the time of writing these items are in the process of being sorted and catalogued by the College Archivist. Their systematic arrangement should in due course provide a valuable body of evidence. There is also manuscript material relating to the servants. The collection of deeds, leases and licences relating to the financial affairs of the estate is enormous, and is supplemented by many letters and papers, again being sorted and catalogued at the present.

Turning to bound manuscript volumes, the most important sources are the Minute Books and the Registers of Applications and Members (the latter concern the out-pensioners as well as the members). There are also Agenda Books, Medical Officers Reports, Obituary Books, Chaplains' Books and Reports, Servants and Nurses Books, etc., all of which have been consulted in the writing of this history: they usually reveal little that is not in the minutes or registers. There is a large range of maps and plans, and some scrapbooks of interesting ephemera. Bound manuscript volumes concerning the financial affairs of the College and estate abound and the most useful of these are mentioned in the notes to the text.

List of Trustees and Officers of Morden College

FROM THE TURKEY COMPANY

Sir Edmund Harrison	1708–1715	James Lee	1770–1806
Sir Pelatiah Barnardiston, Bt.	1708–1712	William Hammond	1774
William Fawkener	1712–1715	John Free	1774
Nicholas Morse	1712–1714	Richard Willis	1777
Philip Papillon	1712–1736	Samuel Bosanquet	1775–1806
Sir Charles Cooke	1712–1720	Peter Cazelet	1785–1787
Thomas Hanger	1712–1733	Richard Clarke	1785–1800
Sir Peter Delme	1716–1729	Edward Forster	1787–1812
Richard Chiswell, M.P.	1716–1744	Nathaniel Free	1788
Thomas Cooke	1721–1752	Thomas Ewer	1789
Kenelm Fawkener	1721–1758	William Cooke	1789–1791
Dudley Foley	1729	Richard M. T. Chiswell, M.P.	1790–1796
Sir John Lock, Bt.	1729–1746	Peter Hammond	1790–1794
John March	1736–1774	William Cazelet	1792
John Cooke	1736	Richard Lee	1795–1798
Richard Chiswell, M.P.	1747–1772	Thomas Farley Forster	1795–1803
William Hanger	1747	Robert Stevenson	1797–1812
Richard Stratton	1750	John Dunnage	1799
Leithullier Tooke	1751–1759	William Bosanquet	1803–1811
James Lock	1751	John Green	1806–1822
William Clark	1759	Jacob Bosanquet	1806–1828
Edward Vernon	1759	William Robinson	1808
Thomas Levett	1759	Sir John Lubbock, Bt.	1809–1815
Puggin Shaw	1759	Sir John William Lubbock, Bt.	1812–1840
William Cooper	1760	William Mellish	1813–1838
Samuel Smith	1764	John Staniforth	1813–1838
William Ewer, M.P.	1766–1789	Edward Lee	1817–1826

FROM THE EAST INDIA COMPANY

William Astell	1827–1847	George Robert Smith	1850–1869
Charles Bosanquet	1827–1850	Thomas Matthias Weguelin, M.P.	1855–1885
James Gibson	1827–1838	Sir John Lubbock, Bt., M.P.	1865–1895
Thomas Warre	1830–1834	Henry Hucks Gibbs, M.P.	1869–1895
Timothy A. Curtis	1839–1855	Jervoise Smith	1874–1884
Thomas Baring, M.P.	1839–1873	*Hon. Ronald Ruthven Leslie-	
Sir J. W. Lubbock, Bt.	1840–1865	Melville, afterwards Earl of	
Lord Leven and Melville	1842–1875	Leven and Melville	1875–1895
Baron John Benjamin Heath	1843–1877	*Henry Burnley Heath	1878–1895
Kirkman Daniel Hodgson, M.P.	1848	*James Stewart Hodgson	1878–1895

*Not Appointed by the East India Company

FROM THE COURT OF ALDERMEN OF THE CITY OF LONDON

Sir Robert Fowler, Bt., M.P., LM 1885–6	1884–1891
Sir Andrew Lusk, Bt., M.P., LM 1873–4	1885–1896
Sir William Lawrence, M.P., LM 1863–4	1891–1895
Sir Joseph C. Dimsdale, Bt., M.D., LM 1901–2	1895–1903
Sir Henry Edmund Knight, LM 1882–3	1895–1910
Sir Reginald Hanson, Bt., M.P., LM 1886–7	1895–1905
Sir David Evans, K.C.M.G., LM 1891–2	1895–1907
Sir Walter Vaughan Morgan, Bt., LM 1905–6	1895
Sir Joseph Savory, Bt., M.P., LM 1890–1	1895
Lt. Col. Sir Horatio D. Davies, K.C.M.G., M.P., LM 1897–8	1896–1912
Sir James T. Ritchie, Bt., LM 1903–4	1903–1912
Sir Walter H. Wilkin, K.C.M.G., LM 1895–6	1905
Sir J. Whittaker Ellis, Bt., M.P., LM 1881–2	1907–1909
Sir Alfred James Newton, Bt., LM 1899–1900	1910
Sir David Burnett, Bt., LM 1912–13	1910
Sir John Charles Bell, Bt., LM 1907–8	1912
Sir Edward E. Cooper, Bt., LM 1919–20	1912
Lord Wakefield of Hythe, LM 1915–16	1916
Sir William Purdie Treloar, Bt., LM 1906–7	1920
Sir T. Vansittart Bowater, Bt., M.P., LM 1913–14	1920
Sir William Henry Dunn, Bt., 1916–17	1921
Lord Marshall of Chipstead, LM 1918–19	1921
Sir James Roll, Bt., LM 1920–1	1921
Sir John James Baddeley, Bt., LM 1921–2	1922
Sir Edward Cecil Moore, Bt., LM 1922–3	1922
Sir Louis Arthur Newton, Bt., LM 1923–4	1923
Sir John Knill, Bt., LM 1909–10	1923
Sir William Robert Pryke, Bt., LM 1925–6	1924
Sir George Wyatt Truscott, Bt., LM 1908–9	1926
Sir Alfred Louis Bower, Bt., LM 1924–5	1927
Sir Charles Albert Batho, Bt., LM 1927–8	1931
Sir Kynaston Studd, Bt., LM 1928–9	1932
Sir Maurice Jenks, Bt., LM 1931–2	1938
Sir Percy W. Greenaway, Bt., LM 1932–3	1938
Sir George Broadbridge, Bt., M.P., LM 1936–7	1940
Sir Harry Twyford, LM 1937–8	1941
Sir John Dawson Laurie, Bt., LM 1941–2	1941
Sir George H. Wilkinson, Bt., LM 1940–1	1944
Sir Frank Newson-Smith, Bt., LM 1943–4	1945
Sir Frank Alexander, Bt., LM 1944–5	1946
Sir Frederick Rowland, LM 1949–50	1947
Sir Charles Davis, Bt., LM 1945–6	1948
Sir Frederick Wells, Bt., LM 1947–8	1950
Sir Bracewell Smith, Bt., LM 1946–7	1952
Sir Noël Vansittart Bowater, Bt., LM 1953–4	1954
Sir Cuthbert Lowell Ackroyd, Bt., LM 1955–6	1958
Sir Denys Lowson, Bt., LM 1950–1	1960
Colonel Sir Cullum Welch, Bt., LM 1956–7	1960

Sir Harold Gillett, Bt.,		Sir Edward Howard, Bt.,	
LM 1958–9	1965	LM 1971–2	1974
Sir James Miller, LM 1964–5	1966	Sir Murray Fox, LM 1974–5	1975
Sir Ralph Perring, Bt.,		Sir Hugh Wontner, LM 1973–4	1976
LM 1962–3	1970	Sir Kenneth Cork, LM 1978–9	1979
Sir Charles Trinder, LM 1968–9	1970	Colonel Sir Ronald Gardner	
Colonel The Rt. Hon. Lord Mais,		Thorpe, LM 1980–1	1979
LM 1972–3	1973		

LM = Lord Mayor of London

TREASURERS

Nathaniel Brand	1708–1729	Horatio Elphinstone Rivers	1872–1901
Joseph Brand	1730–1757	Charles Falkland Monckton	1905–1930
John Bennett	1757–1782	Ernest Paynter	1930–1941
Thomas Bennett	1782–1802	Mr. Cass (Acting Secretary)	1941–1942
Alexander Bennett	1802–1819	Norman Denyer (Acting	
Henry William Smith	1819–1872	Treasurer)	1942–1945

CLERKS TO THE TRUSTEES

Montague S. Graham	1946–1976	Arthur A. Snashall	1976–

CHAPLAINS

Rev. Robert Warren	1701–1702	Rev. William Marsh, Jun.	1842–1862
Rev. Thomas Davies	1702–1705	Rev. William Collett	1862–1865
Rev. Thomas Bowers	1705–1707	Rev. Hon. John Harbord	1865–1892
Rev. Samuel Asplin	1707–1711	Rev. Henry Lansdell	1892–1912
Rev. John Willim	1711–1713	Rev. William Walter Giffard	1912
Rev. John Meredith	1713–1714	Rev. Bertram Henry Meeres	1923
Rev. John Plymley	1714–1759	Rev. John Blakeney King	1927
Rev. Samuel Sandys	1759–1763	Rev. Stewart Sim	1932
Rev. Moses Browne	1763–1787	Rev. Harry Horton	1943
Rev. George Pattrick	1787–1790	Rev. Arthur D. Hodgson	1954
Rev. John Watson	1790–1818	Rev. Thomas E. M. Ashton	1975
Rev. William Marsh, Sen.	1819–1842		

SURVEYORS

Alfred Griffin, F.S.I.	1915–1926	Kenneth B. Leverton, M.B.E.,	
Ernest Paynter, B.Sc., F.S.I.	1926–1941	F.R.I.C.S.	1947–1980
Percy W. Reed, L.R.I.B.A.	1941–1947	Robert V. Chadwick, F.R.I.C.S.	1980–

CHAIRMEN OF TRUSTEES

Sir John William Lubbock, Bt.	1830	Sir T. Vansittart Bowater, Bt.	1923
William Astell	1840	Sir Louis Arthur Newton, Bt.	1938
Sir John Lubbock, Bt.	1847	Sir Maurice Jenks, Bt.	1945
Baron John Benjamin Heath	1865	Lord Broadbridge	1946
Sir John Lubbock, Bt.	1873	Sir Frank Alexander, Bt.	1952
Sir Andrew Lusk, Bt.	1889	Sir Frank Newson-Smith, Bt.	
Sir Henry Edmund Knight	1896	(Acting Chairman)	1959
Sir Joseph Savory, Bt.	1910	Sir Frederick Wells, Bt.	1962
Sir Alfred James Newton, Bt.	1920	Sir Cullum Welch, Bt.	1966
Sir Edward E. Cooper, Bt.	1921	Sir Ralph Perring, Bt.	1979
Sir William Purdie Treloar, Bt.	1922		

(office instituted, 1830)